MW01593724

Jim Burns's work represents his integrity, intelligence, and his heart for kids. The *Uncommon* high school group studies will change some lives and save many others.

stephen arterburn
Bestselling Author, *Every Man's Battle*

Jim Burns has found the right balance between learning God's Word and applying it to life. The topics are relevant, up to date and on target. Jim gets kids to think. This is a terrific series, and I highly recommend it.

les j. christie
Chair of Youth Ministry, William Jessup University, Rocklin, California

There are very few people in the world who know how to communicate life-changing truth effectively to teens. Jim Burns is one of the best. These studies are biblically sound, hands-on practical and just plain fun. This one gets a five-star endorsement.

ken davis
Author and Speaker (www.kendavis.com)

I don't know anyone who knows and understands the needs of the youth worker like Jim Burns. The *Uncommon* high school group studies are solid, easy to use and get students out of their seats and into the Word.

doug fields
Senior Director of HomeWord Center for Youth and Family @ Azusa Pacific University Simply Youth Ministry (www.simplyyouthministry.com)

The practicing youth worker always needs more ammunition. The *Uncommon* high school group studies will get that blank stare off the faces of the kids at your youth meeting!

jay kesler
President Emeritus, Taylor University, Upland, Indiana

In the *Uncommon* high school group studies, Jim Burns pulls together the key ingredients for an effective series. He captures the combination of teen involvement and a solid biblical perspective with topics that are relevant and straightforward. This will be a valuable tool in the local church.

dennis "tiger" mcluen
Executive Director, Youth Leadership (www.youthleadership.com)

Young people need the information necessary to make wise decisions related to everyday problems. The *Uncommon* high school group studies will help many young people integrate their faith into everyday life, which, after all, is our goal as youth workers.

miles mcpherson
Senior Pastor, The Rock Church, San Diego, California

This is a resource that is user-friendly, learner-centered and intentionally biblical. I love having a resource like this that I can recommend to youth ministry volunteers and professionals.

duffy robbins
Professor of Youth Ministry, Eastern University, St. Davids, Pennsylvania

The *Uncommon* high school group studies provide the motivation and information for leaders and the types of experience and content that will capture high school people. I recommend it highly.

denny rydberg
President, Young Life (www.younglife.org)

Jim Burns has done it again! This is a practical, timely and reality-based resource for equipping teens to live life in the fast-paced, pressure-packed adolescent world of today.

rich van pelt
President, Compassion International, Denver, Colorado

Jim Burns has his finger on the pulse of youth today. He understands their mindsets and has prepared these studies in a way that will capture their attention and lead them to greater maturity in Christ.

rick warren
Senior Pastor, Saddleback Church, Lake Forest, California
Author of *The Purpose Driven Life*

uncommon
be extraordinary

high school group study

jim burns

general editor

dealing with stress & crisis

Published by Gospel Light
Ventura, California, U.S.A.
www.gospellight.com
Printed in the U.S.A.

Originally published as *The Word on Helping Friends in Crisis*
by Gospel Light in 1995.

Library of Congress Cataloging-in-Publication Data
Uncommon high school group study & leader's guide : dealing with stress & crisis /
Jim Burns, general editor.
p. cm.
Rev. ed. of: The Word on helping friends in crisis.
Includes bibliographical references and index.
ISBN 978-0-8307-6211-8 (trade paper : alk. paper)
1. Church group work with teenagers. 2. High school students—Conduct of life—
Study and teaching. 3. High school students—Religious life—Study and teaching.
4. Stress in adolescence—Religious aspects—Christianity—Study and teaching.
I. Burns, Jim, 1953- II. Word on helping friends in crisis. III.
Title: Dealing with stress & crisis.
BV4447.U543 2012
268′.433—dc23
2012013609

Rights for publishing this book outside the U.S.A. or in non-English languages are
administered by Gospel Light Worldwide, an international not-for-profit ministry.
For additional information, please visit www.glww.org, e-mail info@glww.org, or write
to Gospel Light Worldwide, 1957 Eastman Avenue, Ventura, CA 93003, U.S.A.

To order copies of this book and other Gospel Light products in bulk quantities,
please contact us at 1-800-446-7735.

dedication

To David Lane

Thank you for your wisdom, counsel and friendship.
You are truly an inspiration.

contents

how to use
the *uncommon*
group bible studies

Each *Uncommon* group Bible study contains 12 sessions, which are divided into 3 stand-alone units of 4 sessions each. You may choose to teach all 12 sessions consecutively, to use just one unit, or to present individual sessions. You know your group, so do what works best for you and your students.

This is your leader's guidebook for teaching your group. Electronic files (in PDF format) of each session's student handouts are available for download at **www.gospellight.com/uncommon/ dealing_with_stress_and_crisis.zip.** The handouts include the "message," "dig," "apply," "reflect" and "meditation" sections of each study and have been formatted for easy printing. You may print as many copies as you need for your group.

Each session opens with a devotional meditation written for you, the youth leader. As hectic and trying as youth work is much of the time, it's important never to neglect your interior life. Use the devotions to refocus your heart and prepare yourself to share with kids the message that has already taken root in you. Each of the 12 sessions are divided into the following sections:

starter

Young people will stay in your youth group if they feel comfortable and make friends in the group. This section is designed for you and the students to get to know each other better.

message

The message section will introduce the Scripture reading for the session and get students thinking about how the passage applies to their lives.

dig

Many young people are biblically illiterate. In this section, students will dig into the Word of God and will begin to interact on a personal level with the concepts.

apply

Young people need the opportunity to think through the issues at hand. This section will get students talking about the passage of Scripture and interacting on important issues.

reflect

The conclusion to the study will allow students to reflect on some of the issues presented in the study on a more personal level.

meditation

A closing Scripture for the students to read and reflect on.

unit I
dealing with stress

I don't know about you, but there is many a day when I feel as if I'm alone. I have to really watch it when I'm under pressure or I become a little moody. And when I'm moody and feel stress coming on, you should see me put down those chocolate chip cookies. Then I look at my stomach and . . . oh, do I feel lonely, worried and moody. At times, that's the real me.

There is a great story from an old children's book called *The Velveteen Rabbit* that captures this idea of "being real." The story begins with a character called the Skin Horse. He had lived longer in the nursery than any of the other toys, and he was so old that his brown coat had become bald in patches (which is how he got his name). The stitching on his seams was showing and most of the hairs on his tail had been pulled out.

One day, a stuffed Rabbit approached the Skin Horse and asked, "What is REAL? Does it mean having things that buzz inside you and a stick-out handle?"

"Real isn't how you are made," replied the Skin Horse. "It's something that happens *to* you. When a child loves you for a long time—not just to play with, but REALLY loves you—then you become Real."

"Does it hurt?" asked the rabbit.

"Sometimes," said the Skin Horse. "But when you are Real, you don't mind being hurt."

"Does it happen all at once, like being wound up," the Rabbit asked, "or bit by bit?"

"It doesn't happen all at once," said the Skin Horse. "You *become*. It takes a long time. That's why it doesn't often happen to people who break easily, or have sharp edges, or who have to be carefully kept. Generally, by the time you are Real, most of your hair has been loved off, your eyes have dropped out and you are loose in the joints and shabby. But these things don't matter at all, because once you are Real, you can't be ugly, except to people who don't understand."[1]

I believe there is a refreshing new wind within many of our churches. Finally, Christians are talking less about being perfect and more about *being real* as they strive to be God's people. Let's be honest. God wants to meet us where we are, not where we should be. Even when we struggle, God is present.

This unit is about taking our Christian faith into the inner struggles of our everyday lives. As an influencer of kids, you can receive the same message that you are presenting in this material—that God loves you just the way you are. So put away any pretenses, relax, and get prepared to offer real answers to real inner struggles.

Note

1. Adapted from Margery Williams, *The Velveteen Rabbit* (New York: Avon Books, 1975), pp. 16-17.

the stress of
loneliness

*The LORD himself goes before you and will be with you; he will never leave
you nor forsake you. Do not be afraid; do not be discouraged.*

DEUTERONOMY 31:8

Loneliness affects just about everyone at times—even leaders. This
is why it is so important that you deal with your own feelings of
loneliness before you try to help our kids, because not dealing
with these feelings will have negative effects on your ministry and
the lives of your teens. If you develop relationships with teenagers
as a way to deal with your loneliness and only have students for
friends, you will create unhealthy relationships and dangerous or
dysfunctional youth ministries.

If you are experiencing loneliness, know that God will walk
with you through that dark valley. You must not allow working
with kids to mask these feelings in your heart. Always remember

that God is with you and your students through the pain and anxiousness that loneliness brings.

So, what can you do if you are lonely? The most effective way of dealing with these feelings is to develop a game plan to counter its ugly effects. In this lesson, you will be inspired to handle personal loneliness in a positive manner and also help your students work through it in a constructive and Christ-centered way. Jesus Himself promised that He would never "leave you as orphans" (John 14:18). He will never abandon you or forsake you. He will walk with you even when you don't feel His presence. His life will overshadow your loneliness with His love and grace.

The best way to forget your own problems is to help others solve theirs.

Anonymous

the stress of loneliness

starter

THE LONELY METER: Divide the group members into team of three to four. Give each person a pen or pencil. Have the group members rate each statement below using a scale of 1 to 10, with 1 being "not lonely at all" and 10 being "extremely lonely."

_____ "When I asked out a person whom I really cared about, he/she told me he/she already had plans."

_____ "My boyfriend/girlfriend broke up with me on Friday and went out with another girl/guy on Saturday."

_____ "I spilled my tray of food in front of everyone in the cafeteria. I feel like a total loser!"

Note: You can download this group study guide in 8½" x 11" format at **www.gospellight.com/uncommon/dealing_with_stress_and_crisis.zip.**

_____ "We all went to the amusement park and had a pretty good time."

_____ "We had the best talk."

_____ "I couldn't find anyone who wanted to go to the movies on Friday."

_____ "I have a good friend at school, and we do lots of things together."

_____ "My Christmas was horrible—the first since my parents divorced. My dad went out drinking and my mom went on a date. I sat home all by myself."

Now have the group members indicate whether they believe the statements below are mostly true or mostly false:

True	False	The majority of people in my school are lonely most of the time.
True	False	Adults tend to be lonelier than teenagers.
True	False	Loneliness causes people to lower their moral standards.
True	False	Some teenagers have sex, become pregnant and get married because they are lonely.
True	False	God can always cure a person's loneliness.

When everyone is finished, gather back together and ask the teams to share their responses. Ask the group members to share any other "lonely statements" they would like to add to this list.

message

The Bible is full of truths that God wants us to understand, and one of these truths is that we are never alone. God is always with us. As we see in Psalm 23, God watches over everything we do, and He knows exactly what we are going through:

> *The LORD is my shepherd, I shall not be in want. He makes me lie down in green pastures, he leads me beside quiet waters, he restores my soul. He guides me in paths of righteousness for his name's sake. Even though I walk through the valley of the shadow of death, I will fear no evil, for you are with me; your rod and your staff, they comfort me. You prepare a table before me in the presence of my enemies. You anoint my head with oil; my cup overflows. Surely goodness and love will follow me all the days of my life, and I will dwell in the house of the LORD forever.*

1. According to this psalm, God is our "shepherd." What are some of the things He does for us as our shepherd?

    He makes me_____ _____ in green pastures.

    He _____ me beside _____ _____.

    He _____ my _____.

    He _____ me in _____ of _____.

2. What are some of the places this psalm says God is with us?

    _____

    _____

    _____

3. What do you think "the darkest valley" could represent in a person's life?

    _____

    _____

    _____

4. Why should a person not be afraid when he or she encounters these places?

    _____

    _____

    _____

5. "You prepare a table before me" refers to someone setting a table for a feast. Why does the location for this feast seem strange?

    _____

    _____

    _____

6. What is used to anoint the person?

    _____

    _____

    _____

7. What do you think the term "my cup overflows," means?

    _____

    _____

    _____

8. What two things will follow us all the days of our lives?

    _____

    _____

    _____

9. Where will we dwell forever?

    _____

    _____

    _____

dig

Throughout the Bible, God uses this illustration of a shepherd to help us understand what He means when He says He is always with us. For example, in Isaiah 40:11 we read, "He tends his flock like a shepherd: He gathers the lambs in his arms and carries them close to his heart; he gently leads those that have young." However, because so few of us know anything about what a shepherd does, we can easily miss the significance of what God is saying. So let's take a closer look at the shepherding process.

the shepherd

We'll begin by looking at a few of the qualities and characteristics of the shepherd.

1. Let's say you are a sheep owner. You start with 30 sheep. In 10 years, what will happen to the amount of sheep that you have?

   _____

   _____

   _____

2. Now say you have 100 sheep and 1 small meadow behind your house. What will happen to that meadow in a short amount of time? Why will this be a problem for you and your sheep?

   _____

   _____

   _____

As you've probably have guessed, your flock of sheep would grow over time and the amount of grazing land would be much less than you need to feed your growing flock. You would need to expand where the sheep feed—and you would need to find help watching a flock of this size. You could solve the problem by putting someone from your family in charge of the sheep (a shepherd). Because the shepherd would be a member of your family, that person would know how important it is to take good care of the sheep.

3. One of the shepherd's jobs was to move the flock through wilderness areas from meadow to meadow so there would always be enough food. The shepherd would also make sure the sheep had water and see that they were protected. From what types of things do you think a shepherd would need to protect the flock?

4. To protect the sheep, the shepherd had to be with them 24/7. Why do you think this was important?

A shepherd had to constantly watch his flock. If the weather became too hot, he would have to move his flock to a cooler place. If one of the sheep went missing, he would have to find that sheep and bring it back to the flock. If one of the sheep needed medical attention, he had to be the veterinarian who would treat the sheep. If a wild animal decided it wanted one of the sheep for dinner, the shepherd would have to fight it off to keep the sheep safe.

the sheep

Now let's look at a bit more closely at the sheep. Sheep need a leader from among the flock. They don't care who the leader is, as long as some sheep—any sheep—does the job. Sometimes, the leader of a flock is the first sheep that decides to move forward, and all the other sheep get behind that one. This instinct to follow is so strong that people tend to think sheep are stupid; however, they are actually fairly smart. Sheep have long-term facial recognition, which means they can learn to recognize the face of their shepherd. [2]

1. What are some benefits of the sheep's instinct to follow?

    _____

    _____

    _____

2. What are some of the drawbacks of this instinct?

    _____

    _____

    _____

    _____

3. Why is long-term facial recognition important if you are a sheep?

    _____

    _____

    _____

A sheep's ability to recognize its shepherd's face often means the difference between life and death. When the sheep sees the shepherd, it knows and follows that person—the one who is always with it, always protects it, and always provides for all its needs. The sheep finds security and comfort in the presence of the shepherd.

apply

In John 10:14, Jesus said, "I am the good shepherd; I know my sheep and my sheep know me." Like any good shepherd, Jesus is always there for His "sheep" (us), protecting them and providing for their needs. He has promised to never leave us: "Surely I am with you always, to the very end of the age" (Matthew 28:20). Jesus knows when we are feeling lonely, and He wants us to know that He is always there beside us.

1. Can you remember a specific time in your life when you were lonely? Explain.

    ----

2. Circle the letter below that best describes what you are most likely to do when you are feeling lonely:

    a. Go into your bedroom and crank up your music
    b. Call your best friend and tell him/her how you feel
    c. Go to the mall and start conversations with all the people you can find who are your age (or at least don't look scary)
    d. Start doing something—alphabetize your music collection, bake all the recipes from your international cook-book, paint the walls of your bedroom, or run five miles

3. How do these things help you to feel not so lonely?

    ----

4. Jesus wants to be your shepherd even in the darkest times of your life. Look at each of the situations below. How would knowing that Jesus is your shepherd change in the way you handle them? In other words, what difference would it make to know that Jesus is right there with you and helping you?

    a. Your dad just lost his job, and your family might have to move to another state.

    b. You find out that you have diabetes and will need to get several shots every day for the rest of your life.

    c. Your best friend just got in trouble with the police for shoplifting.

    d. A close family member was just diagnosed with cancer.

5. The following are seven statements about loneliness. Answer
    whether or not you think each statement is true, and why you
    think this way.

    a. Everyone experiences loneliness.

    _____

    _____

    _____

    b. Sometimes loneliness can be helpful.

    _____

    _____

    _____

    c. When you are lonely, it isn't healthy to withdraw from
        everyone and everything.

    _____

    _____

    _____

6. Now here are a few things you can do when you are lonely. Af-
    ter each idea, write down one practical way you could put this
    into practice the next time you are feeling this way.

    a. *Take a risk.* Reach out to others and develop friendships.

    _____

    _____

    _____

    b. *Enjoy yourself.* When you feel the lonely bug come over
        you, do something you enjoy, such as going for a walk, read-

ing a good book, writing a letter, reading the Bible (Psalms and Proverbs can be especially helpful), treating yourself to a movie, or calling a friend and having fun together.

_____

_____

_____

c. *Be others-centered.* Do something that takes the focus off yourself and the way you are feeling and begin to focus on the needs of others.

_____

_____

_____

d. *Talk to the Shepherd.* Talk to Jesus about your loneliness and ask Him to be your closest friend.

_____

_____

_____

reflect

1. Turn once more to Psalm 23. What does each of the following statements mean in terms of how God has promised to care for you, be with you, and watch over you?

"I shall not be in want" (verse 1)

_____

_____

_____

_____

"He restores my soul" (verse 3)

"He guides me in paths of righteousness" (verse 3)

"Even though I walk through the valley of the shadow of death,
I will fear no evil, for you are with me" (verse 4)

----

2. Psalm 23:4 states, "Your rod and your staff, they comfort me."
    In biblical times, shepherds used a rod (a long stick) not only
    to protect their sheep but also to discipline them when they
    wandered their own way. Why do you think David would say
    that this gave him comfort?

----

3. The shepherd's staff was a long and slender stick with a hook
    on one end. A shepherd used this item to reach out and catch
    a sheep so he could bring it closer to himself and to guide it

down a difficult path. In what ways do you think David would consider this to be a comfort?

---

4. In Psalm 23:5, David writes, "You serve me a six-course dinner right in front of my enemies" (*THE MESSAGE*). Why would God want your enemies to see this? What would it do to them? How would it help you?

---

5. Who are some people in your life that you would like to become closer friends with? List three or four names.

---

6. What could you do with each person during the next two weeks to strengthen your relationship (for example, have lunch together, go shopping, go bike riding)?

---

7. Make a list of five special things you like to do. (Keep this list
    handy, and the next time you feel lonely, read through it and
    do one or more of the things you have suggested.)

    _____

    _____

    _____

8. What can you do to become a more others-centered person?
    List several service-oriented things you can do. Be as specific
    as possible (for example, bake cookies for Grandma, mow the
    lawn this afternoon, write an encouraging note to someone).

    _____

    _____

    _____

    _____

9. Close by taking some time now to talk to God. Let Him know
    how you feel and what you need. Write down anything He
    tells you or any feelings you have about Him.

    _____

    _____

    _____

    _____

meditation

*Where can I go from your Spirit? Where can I flee from
your presence? If I go up to the heavens, you are there; if I make
my bed in the depths, you are there.*

PSALM 139:7-8

the stress of mood swings

Answer me quickly, O LORD; my spirit fails. Do not hide your face from me or I will be like those who go down to the pit. Let the morning bring me word of your unfailing love, for I have put my trust in you. Show me the way I should go, for to you I lift up my soul.

PSALM 143:7-8

The teenage years can be some of the most difficult because of the mood swings teenagers experience. Even a mild-mannered child can become moody when puberty hits. Teens can be happy one moment and irritable and whiny the next. Their constantly changing hormones make it difficult for them to deal with life's challenges in a balanced way, and sometimes the littlest thing can seem trigger a different mood. So, how do you deal with moody teens?

First, *find out what is going on in a teenager's life*. Family problems, medical issues, abuses and traumas will understandably trigger a negative mood in a teenager, especially if he or she doesn't have the support to deal with it. This can come out as anger, sadness, withdrawal and irritability, among other emotions.

Next, *teach and model the fact that though humans change all the time, God never changes*. He is the rock of their lives and will always be there for them. When they feel as if everything in their world is changing, God will be the same loving and accepting Father they need. When you love your students in their good moods and in bad, it builds trust into your relationships and shows them what God is like.

Finally, *help teens see that their attitudes and actions are a choice—a choice that only they can make*. When they are moody, they are choosing to let their hormones and life situations control them. They have the power in Jesus to make a choice not to let their situations cause them to sink emotionally. They can choose to remember that God loves them and will never fail them. They can choose to change their attitudes.

It may also be helpful to put yourself through the process of examining what makes *you* moody and then figuring out what you need to do to change your negative attitude. This is also a good time to saturate yourself in verses that speak of God's faithfulness, constancy and unchanging nature. As you begin to work through your moodiness, you will be able to help your teens.

Perhaps the greatest discovery of this century is that if you can change your attitude, you can change your life.
WILLIAM JAMES

the stress of mood swings

starter

PET PEEVES: Gather the group members together into teams of three or four people and ask them to answer the following questions in their groups:

1. What are my two greatest pet peeves?
2. What is one thing in my life that I really don't like?
3. If I could change something about my family, what would it be?
4. When I become an adult, what will I let teenagers do?
5. If I were the person in charge of teenagers, what would I do?

Ask volunteers to share their responses and describe the attitudes/moods that accompany their feelings about each question. Explain that we all have moods and attitudes that pull us down at times, which are influenced by a number of different factors. Recognizing how our emotions affect us can help us manage our feelings in healthy ways.

message

King David was an emotional man. He was also an honest man. When you read through the psalms he wrote, you can see his emotional ups and downs—and there were some pretty serious mood triggers going on in his life as well. However, David found the key to dealing with his emotions and trials through his solid relationship with God. He knew that no matter what happened, God would always be there to help him. He knew God would always be faithful to him, even when he wasn't so faithful in return.

grateful for God's faithfulness

One psalm that David wrote to express his gratitude to God for His faithfulness was Psalm 145:

> *I will exalt you, my God the King; I will praise your name for ever and ever. Every day I will praise you and extol your name for ever and ever. . . . Your kingdom is an everlasting kingdom, and your dominion endures through all generations. The LORD is faithful to all his promises and loving toward all he has made. The LORD upholds all those who fall and lifts up all who are bowed down. . . . The LORD is righteous in all his ways and loving toward all he has made. The LORD is near to all who call on him, to all who call on him in truth.*

1. What are some words in this psalm that lead you to believe God is going to be around for a long time—forever, in fact?

    ....

    ....

    ....

    ....

2. According to these verses, when God promises to do something, can you trust that He will do it? Why?

    ....

    ....

    ....

    ....

3. Look at the verses below. After each one, write down how God shows His people He is faithful and worthy of trust.

    For in the day of trouble he will keep me safe in his dwelling; he will hide me in the shelter of his tabernacle and set me high upon a rock (Psalm 27:5).

    ....

    ....

    ....

    ....

    And my God will meet all your needs according to his glorious riches in Christ Jesus (Philippians 4:19).

    ....

    ....

    ....

    ....

God so loved the world that he gave his one and only Son, that who-
ever believes in him shall not perish but have eternal life (John 3:16).

---

the faithful father

Another example of God's faithful love is found in a parable Jesus told in Luke 15:11-24:

There was a man who had two sons. The younger one said to his
father, "Father, give me my share of the estate." So he divided his
property between them.

Not long after that, the younger son got together all he had, set
off for a distant country and there squandered his wealth in wild
living. After he had spent everything, there was a severe famine in
that whole country, and he began to be in need. So he went and
hired himself out to a citizen of that country, who sent him to his
fields to feed pigs. He longed to fill his stomach with the pods that
the pigs were eating, but no one gave him anything.

When he came to his senses, he said, "How many of my fa-
ther's hired men have food to spare, and here I am starving to
death! I will set out and go back to my father and say to him: Fa-
ther, I have sinned against heaven and against you. I am no longer
worthy to be called your son; make me like one of your hired
men." So he got up and went to his father.

But while he was still a long way off, his father saw him and
was filled with compassion for him; he ran to his son, threw his
arms around him and kissed him.

The son said to him, "Father, I have sinned against heaven
and against you. I am no longer worthy to be called your son."

But the father said to his servants, "Quick! Bring the best robe and put it on him. Put a ring on his finger and sandals on his feet. Bring the fattened calf and kill it. Let's have a feast and celebrate. For this son of mine was dead and is alive again; he was lost and is found."

1. What did the son ask the father to give him in the beginning of the parable?

    _____

    _____

    _____

2. What did the younger son do with the money? What happened as a result?

    _____

    _____

    _____

3. What happened in the country where he went to live?

    _____

    _____

    _____

4. How would you describe the mood of the younger son?

    _____

    _____

    _____

5. What made him finally decide to return home to his father?

    _____

    _____

    _____

6. What happens when the son gets close to his father's home? What do you think the father was doing in order to see the son "while he was still a long way off"?

---

7. How do you think the younger son see himself at this point?

---

8. What do the actions of the father say about his character and how he sees his son?

---

dig

The word "faithful" means "having or showing true and constant support or loyalty; deserving trust; keeping your promises or doing what you are supposed to do."[1] Given this definition, one opposite of faithfulness would be moodiness. Our moods change constantly, so they are very unreliable for us to use when making decisions. However, faithfulness is a reflection of God's character that exists in *spite* of our moods. Faithfulness will help us weather life's storms regardless of what we are feeling.

1. Consider the parable of the lost son that Jesus told in Luke 15:11-24. If the father represents God and the younger son represents us, which of the following indicate how God sees us when our emotions and impulses pull us away from Him?

   ❑ He gets upset and tells us to snap out of it.
   ❑ He feels disappointed that we can't seem to get our emotions under control.
   ❑ He loves us and is always there with His arms opened wide no matter what mood we are in.
   ❑ He no longer trusts us and keeps us at a distance.

2. In Psalm 145:13, David writes, "The LORD is faithful to all his promises and loving toward all he has made. The LORD upholds all those who fall and lifts up all who are bowed down." Let's say you make a bad decision and you "fall." Based on this verse, which of the following would likely be God's response to you?

   ❑ God leaves you on your own with the parting words, "I told you so! Maybe next time you'll listen to Me!"
   ❑ God is so embarrassed by your mistake that He pretends not to know you.
   ❑ God runs to you and scoops you up in His arms.
   ❑ God laughs at you for being so foolish.

3. Put a *T* next to the statements you think are true and an *F* next to the ones you think are false.

   ___ The Lord only acts righteously toward people who do good.
   ___ The Lord is always faithful regardless of the situation.
   ___ The Lord is righteous no matter what.

___ If you call on the Lord for help, it had better be an emergency or He will be angry with you.

___ The Lord is faithful only to those who have faith in Him.

___ The Lord is near to a person who calls to Him in truth.

4. Based on the verses we have studied so far, how can we know
    that God is the same yesterday, today and forever?

    _____

    _____

    _____

apply

Throughout the Bible, God shows that He is always faithful to
those who put their trust in Him. As David writes, "Surely God is
my help; the Lord is the one who sustains me" (Psalm 54:4). But
there will be others in our lives who will be less helpful when we
are feeling moody or depressed, as the following skit illustrates.
Read this skit to yourself or act it out as part of a group.

the no-help helpers

Cast: Moody Kid, Visitor #1, Visitor #2, Visitor #3
Time: The present
Place: Moody Kid's home

(As the skit begins, Moody Kid is sitting on a chair in the front of
the room facing center stage. He is looking down and frowning.
He remains this way throughout the skit.)

Visitor #1: Hey, c'mon. We're all going to the game. (Pulls on
    Moody Kid's arm.) What's the matter with you? You're no

fun anymore. Well, if that's the way you feel, we'll just go without you. (Visitor #1 leaves. Moody Kid moves his chair a bit to the right.)

Visitor #2: What've you got to be miserable about, anyway? Now Ted—*he's* got problems. Andrea dumped him, he's failing math and he got cut from the basketball team. So snap out of it! (Visitor #2 waves her hand in disgust and walks off. Moody Kid moves his chair a bit more to the right, so that he is sitting sideways to the audience.)

Visitor #3: Hey, don't you know that good Christians don't have mood swings? If you'd just pray and read your Bible, you'd be fine. I'm never moody, and it's all because I'm a Christian. (Visitor #3 walks off, nose in the air. Moody Kid again moves his chair to the right, to the point that his back faces the audience.)

1. Based on Moody Kid's body language, how do you think he or she was feeling?

   _____

   _____

   _____

   _____

   _____

2. What assumptions did each visitor make? Why wasn't their advice helpful?

   _____

   _____

   _____

   _____

3. How do you want friends to treat you if you are feeling moody?

_____

_____

_____

God loves us and accepts us the way we are. He is waiting to help us, but He asks us to choose to participate in handling our moods. When we feel moody, we can choose to allow our emotions to overwhelm us, causing us to withdraw, be fearful, angry and distrustful of God; or we can turn to God—who is always there for us—and trust that He will take care of us. Along with prayer and digging into God's Word, God will also use people in our lives—such as a Christian friend, a parent, a pastor or a counselor—to help us. If negative moods persist, we can get feedback from some of these people.

triggers and symptoms of mood swings
To better understand our mood swings, it is helpful to look at some of the things that occur that often trigger them. Place an *X* or checkmark beside any of the following that you have experienced recently:

- ❑ Academic problems
- ❑ Alcohol abuse by family member(s)
- ❑ Physical and emotional changes associated with puberty and adolescence
- ❑ Domestic violence
- ❑ Drug abuse by family member(s)
- ❑ Emotional or psychological problems of family member(s)
- ❑ Excessive discipline
- ❑ Family tensions
- ❑ Fear of failure
- ❑ Illness or death of a close friend
- ❑ Illness or death of a family member
- ❑ Inadequate housing
- ❑ Inconsistent discipline
- ❑ Lack of effective communication between family members

- ❏ Living in a dangerous neighborhood
- ❏ Living in a single-parent household
- ❏ Moving/changing schools
- ❏ One or both parents are frequently absent from home
- ❏ Overcrowding at home
- ❏ Parental issues
- ❏ Parental separation or divorce
- ❏ Peer pressures
- ❏ Personal health problems
- ❏ Personal setbacks, disappointments or embarrassments
- ❏ Physical deformities
- ❏ Physical or emotional neglect
- ❏ Physical, sexual or psychological abuse
- ❏ Racism
- ❏ Rejection by family members, friends, peers or others
- ❏ School or athletic performance anxieties
- ❏ Sexual impulses
- ❏ Unrealistic parental expectations or demands
- ❏ Unrealistic teacher expectations or demands

Now place an X or checkmark beside any of the following symptoms you have experienced recently:

- ❏ Aggressiveness
- ❏ Anxiety
- ❏ Apathy
- ❏ Biting nails
- ❏ Boredom
- ❏ Clenching jaws
- ❏ Constipation
- ❏ Crying
- ❏ Depression
- ❏ Diarrhea
- ❏ Dizziness
- ❏ Eating disorders
- ❏ Excessive frustration
- ❏ Grinding teeth
- ❏ Habitual clearing of throat
- ❏ Headaches
- ❏ Hostility
- ❏ Inattention
- ❏ Insecurity
- ❏ Lethargy
- ❏ Loss of confidence
- ❏ Loud or rapid speech
- ❏ Mood swings
- ❏ Muscle aches
- ❏ Nightmares
- ❏ Nit-picking
- ❏ Pacing or wandering
- ❏ Picking at skin
- ❏ Panicky fears
- ❏ Persistent fatigue
- ❏ Poor concentration

❑ Poor self-esteem
❑ Rapid heartbeat
❑ Rashes and other skin disorders
❑ Restlessness
❑ Rudeness or use of shocking language
❑ Self-neglect
❑ Short-term memory loss
❑ Silence
❑ Stomachaches
❑ Stuttering
❑ Suicidal thoughts, gestures or attempts
❑ Tapping fingers or feet
❑ Teary-eyedness
❑ Tics or twitches
❑ Ulcers
❑ Unexplained irritability
❑ Unpreparedness
❑ Unusual perspiring
❑ Use/abuse of alcohol or other drugs
❑ Violence
❑ Withdrawal
❑ Worrying

coping with mood swings

Remember that addressing your mood swings requires a conscious choice on your part. God won't force you into action or magically remove a negative attitude without your permission—though He will be there to help and guide you along the way. So, when your emotions seem to be raging out of control, review the mood-swing triggers list above to see what might be causing the problem, and then watch for any of the symptoms. In addition, it is important to guard yourself against these attacks.

1. Read Ephesians 6:10-18. How are we supposed to fight against things that attack us?

   _____

   _____

   _____

2. God gives us spiritual "armor" so we can stand firm and remember His faithfulness when we are under attack. Which of

the pieces of armor that Paul listed do you most need to equip right now? Why?

_____

_____

_____

_____

3. If we are using God's power and are wearing His armor, whose fight is this?

_____

_____

_____

4. Another thing you can do when you are feeling moody is to expose yourself to God's positive input. According to Philippians 4:8, on what types of things are you to focus your mind?

    whatever is _____
    whatever is _____
    whatever is _____
    whatever is _____
    whatever is _____
    whatever is _____
    anything [that] is _____ or _____

5. Choose one of the items from this list. What are some practical habits you could develop to start focusing your mind more on this thing?

_____

_____

_____

6. Finally, when mood swings hit, you can (and *should*) ask God for help. The psalmist understood this well when he wrote, "O LORD, the God who saves me, day and night I cry out before you" (Psalm 88:1). What is one situation in your life right now that is causing your emotions to go out of control?

    _____

    _____

    _____

7. Have you prayed about this situation? If not, write a short note to God asking Him for help. Remember that when you ask Him honestly, He will be there to help you!

    _____

    _____

    _____

    _____

reflect

As you conclude this study, remember that there is no situation that is too big for God to handle. Also remember that God loves you just the way you are—even when you are moody—and He wants to help you deal with your emotions.

1. Think about a stressful situation in the past that made your moods swing out of control. Do you remember having any physical symptoms (nausea, headache and so on) at the time? If so, what were they?

    _____

    _____

    _____

2. What was going on inside you? How did you feel emotionally?

3. Did you try to let go of the negative emotions and give them to God? If so, what did you do? What was the result?

4. Did you have a friend come beside you for support? If so, what did that person do to help you through this tough time?

5. How did you see God at work through this experience?

6. If you were facing this same situation today, what would you do differently to handle it?

7. Do you have a friend who is moody? If so, how can you help
    that person?

    _____

    _____

    _____

    _____

    _____

meditation

*As for God, his way is perfect; the word of the LORD is flawless.
He is a shield for all who take refuge in him. For who is God besides
the LORD? And who is the Rock except our God? It is God who arms
me with strength and makes my way perfect.*

PSALM 18:30-32

Notes

1. Merriam-Webster Learner's Dictionary, s.v. "faithful." http://www.learnersdictionary.com/
    search/faithful.
2. *When Kids Have Personal Problems* (Elgin, IL: David C. Cook Publishing, 1991), p. 13-A. Used
    by permission.

the stress of worry

Search me, O God, and know my heart; test me and know my anxious thoughts.
See if there is any offensive way in me, and lead me in the way everlasting.

PSALM 139:23-24

Worry is a problem for most people in our country. The thing is that we usually worry about the wrong things. What we really should be worried about is being worried.

God created our bodies to respond to danger. When we encounter something dangerous, our bodies automatically go into "safety" mode. Our bodies fill up with adrenaline and other hormones that prepare it for action—to fight the danger or run away from it. Blood rushes to our arms and legs so that we can take action. Our heart rate increases, and so does our breathing.

All this would be fine if we actually needed to run or fight. However, because so much of what we worry about has to do with things such as problem solving, negotiating, and so on, instead we end up sitting at our desks or pacing up and down a hallway.

All that adrenaline pumping, blood rushing and heart rate increasing begins to have a negative effect on us. We start to feel new aches and pains. Our digestive systems begin to malfunction. We develop high blood pressure or insomnia. If we continue to worry over a long period of time, these unhealthy chemicals in our bodies can take a toll on our organs and our immune system.[1]

Worry is not good for us, nor is it good for your group members. God says over and over again in the Bible not to worry (see Matthew 6:25-27,34; Luke 12:25; John 14:27; Philippians 4:6). So we all need to stop worrying.

Working with teenagers is a great way to become others-centered, and it's a healthy alternative to focusing on your worries. Although finances, relational problems, work conflicts, inner struggles and health concerns can sap your emotional energy, serving young people as a sign of your devotion to the Lord can bring an eternal perspective to your present circumstances.

Before you begin the lesson today, spend some time studying passages in the Bible that refer to worry and God's peace. Present all your worries, anxieties and concerns to God. Lay everything in His hands. Then praise Him for His faithfulness and love for you. God promises His peace and presence to those who ask for it.

Never worry about anything that is past. Charge it up to experience and forget the trouble. There are always plenty of troubles ahead, so don't turn and look back on any behind you.

HERBERT HOOVER

Note
1. Rosalind Ryan, "What Worrying Does to Your Health," MailOnline. http://www.dailymail.co.uk/health/article-97853/What-worrying-does-health.html.

the stress of worry

starter

WORRY-O-METER: Make copies of the Worry-O-Meter found at **www.gospellight.com/uncommon/dealing_with_stress_and_crisis.zip** and give one to each person in your group. Instruct them to write a number next to each of the potential stressful situations below on a scale of 1 to 10, with 10 meaning they worry about it all of the time and a 1 meaning they worry little about it.

message

Some people seem to worry about everything—even things that are unlikely to ever happen to them. Others worry about very real and pressing situations that they are experiencing in their lives. What does God say about worry?

don't be anxious about anything

In fact, in the Bible God tells us that He doesn't want us to worry about *anything*. In Philippians 4:6-7, Paul writes:

> *Do not be anxious about anything, but in everything, by prayer and petition, with thanksgiving, present your requests to God. And the peace of God, which transcends all understanding, will guard your hearts and your minds in Christ Jesus.*

1. In this passage, Paul tells us *not* to be anxious. He also tells us *to do* something. What are we to do instead of being anxious?

---

2. How would you define the following words?

Prayer

Petition

Thanksgiving

---

3. According to these verses, if we have an issue that is making us anxious we should:

   ❏ Write a list of 120 ways we might be able to fix it
   ❏ Present it to God
   ❏ Block out the thoughts and try to forget the problem by playing our favorite computer game
   ❏ Eat a carton of double-chocolate-fudge-brownie ice cream

4. According to Philippians 4:6-7, what will God provide when we give our worries to Him?

   _____

   _____

   _____

   _____

5. What kind of "peace" do you think Paul is talking about here?

   _____

   _____

   _____

do not worry about tomorrow

When you read the Bible, you will continually see terms such as "do not worry" or "do not be afraid." God knows that as human beings, it is in our nature to worry, and throughout His Word He reassures us that He has everything under control. Consider Jesus' words in Matthew 6:25-34:

> *Therefore I tell you, do not worry about your life, what you will eat or drink; or about your body, what you will wear. Is not life more important than food, and the body more important than clothes? Look at the birds of the air; they do not sow or reap or store*

away in barns, and yet your heavenly Father feeds them. Are you not much more valuable than they? Who of you by worrying can add a single hour to his life? And why do you worry about clothes? See how the lilies of the field grow. They do not labor or spin. Yet I tell you that not even Solomon in all his splendor was dressed like one of these. If that is how God clothes the grass of the field, which is here today and tomorrow is thrown into the fire, will he not much more clothe you, O you of little faith? So do not worry, saying, "What shall we eat?" or "What shall we drink?" or "What shall we wear?" For the pagans run after all these things, and your heavenly Father knows that you need them. But seek first his kingdom and his righteousness, and all these things will be given to you as well. Therefore do not worry about tomorrow, for tomorrow will worry about itself. Each day has enough trouble of its own.

1. What are some of the things Jesus mentions in this passage about which we are not to worry?

   _____

   _____

   _____

2. How does Jesus say that God will respond to the needs we often worry about?

   _____

   _____

   _____

3. In one portion of this passage, Jesus refers to the lilies of the field and states "not even Solomon in all his splendor was dressed like one of these." To a Jewish person Solomon's court represented the pinnacle of human glory, yet Jesus says not

even he was dressed as well as the lilies of the field. What point
was Jesus making here when he said "they do not labor or spin"?

_____

_____

_____

4. What contrast does Jesus make between us and the "the grass
    of the field"? What does this say about how God values us?

    _____

    _____

    _____

5. What does Jesus tell us to do instead of focusing on problems?

    _____

    _____

    _____

dig

Because the tendency to worry is universal, it will take practice,
trust in God and a determination to follow His advice to overcome worry. We can't always control our circumstances, but we
can, with God's help, control how we respond to those circumstances and how we allow them to shape us.

1. In Philippians 4:7, Paul says that when you take your concerns
    to God, He will give you peace and guard your heart. In what
    ways has God given you peace in a stressful situation?

    _____

    _____

    _____

2. How has God protected and guarded you in the past? What does this tell you about whether or not you can trust Him in any situation?

   _____

   _____

   _____

   _____

3. The following phrases come from Matthew 6:25-34. What does it mean in your life to worry about each of these things?

   your life . . .

   _____

   _____

   _____

   what you will eat or drink . . .

   _____

   _____

   _____

   your body . . .

   _____

   _____

   _____

   what you will wear . . .

   _____

   _____

   _____

4. How does Jesus portray God in this passage? What do we know about God's character from reading these verses?

    _____

    _____

    _____

    _____

5. What kind of person does God want to help you become? How does He help you accomplish this? (Note: If you want to know what it means to know God as a loving heavenly Father, talk to a Christian friend or pastor. Being part of the family has its perks!)

    _____

    _____

    _____

    _____

6. Instead of worrying, God asks you to seek His kingdom and His righteousness. What does this mean to you? How can you do this?

    _____

    _____

    _____

    _____

7. What does Jesus say will happen to a person who first seeks God's kingdom and His righteousness?

    _____

    _____

    _____

    _____

apply

1. The word "worry" has an interesting history. It comes from the Old English word *wyrgan*, which literally meant "to strangle." In the mid-1500s, people used the word to describe how dogs or wolves attacked a flock of sheep: "to harass by rough or severe treatment."[1] Given this definition, when you worry, what are you really doing to yourself?

    _____

    _____

    _____

    _____

2. Over time, how do you think treating yourself in this way will affect your body? Your mind? Your emotions?

    _____

    _____

    _____

    _____

3. How does worrying affect a person's ability to trust God?

    _____

    _____

    _____

4. In what way is trusting God and having faith in Him to provide for you the exact opposite of worry?

    _____

    _____

    _____

    _____

5. What do you tend to worry about the most? What are you focused on when you worry about these things?

6. Have you ever tried to stop worrying about something that was really bothering you? If you succeeded, how did you do it?

7. What helps you to focus on God when you have a troubling situation in your life?

8. In Philippians 3:13-14, Paul says, "Forgetting what is behind and straining toward what is ahead, I press on toward the goal." Why is this attitude healthy?

9. Proverbs 23:7 states, "For as [a man] thinks in his heart, so is he" (*NKJV*). How does this proverb relate to the idea of overcoming worry in your life?

10. In 1 Thessalonians 5:18, Paul writes, "Give thanks in all circumstances, for this is God's will for you in Christ Jesus." Being thankful is one way we seek God's kingdom and His righteousness. It often starts as an action, but with time it can become an attitude. What do you think is the first step to becoming more thankful?

_____

_____

_____

11. How can you learn to be thankful in "all circumstances"?

_____

_____

_____

12. Proverbs 3:5-6 states, "Trust in the LORD with all your heart and lean not on your own understanding; in all your ways acknowledge him, and he will make your paths straight." What are some ways you can trust and acknowledge God in all things?

_____

_____

_____

_____

reflect

1. How do you think worry and stress can hinder you from getting your day-to-day tasks completed?

_____

_____

_____

2. How can worry and stress affect your relationship with God?

    _____

    _____

    _____

3. Have you ever literally made yourself sick with worry? Explain.

    _____

    _____

    _____

    _____

4. In Psalm 37, David provides some good advice on the topic of
    fretting (or worrying). Fill in the blanks below:

    Do not _____ because of _____ _____ (verse 1).
    _____ in the Lord and do _____ (verse 3).
    _____ yourself in the Lord (verse 4).
    _____ your way to the Lord; _____ in him (verse 5).

5. What would be the results of following this advice?

    _____

    _____

    _____

    _____

6. What worries in your life today do you need to give to God?

    _____

    _____

    _____

    _____

7. First Peter 5:7 states, "Cast all your anxiety on [God] because he cares for you." So, right now write to God and ask Him to take all of your anxieties away from you. Ask Him for help in your situation, and write down anything He has taught you about worry as well.

    _____

    _____

    _____

    _____

    _____

8. What benefits of *not* worrying do you want to have in your life?

    _____

    _____

    _____

    _____

    _____

meditation

And we know that in all things God works for the good of those who love him, who have been called according to his purpose.

ROMANS 8:28

Note

1. *The Online Etymology Dictionary*, definition for "worry." http://www.etymonline.com.

the stress of negative self-image

In 1998, a company called The Body Shop started a campaign against the unrealistic body image being portrayed to kids through the Barbie doll. They created posters of a Barbie doll using the correct proportions of most women in America, and under the picture they put the words, "There are three billion women who don't look like supermodels and only eight who do."

In fact, it has been said that if the Barbie doll were a real woman, she would be five feet nine inches tall, have a neck that was double the length of a normal person, and weigh 110 pounds. This means she would be under the healthy weight for a woman and suffer from a number of internal issues. She would also not be able to walk, because her feet would be too small to support her body.

The Barbie doll isn't the only offender. Take a look at action figures. Male action figures usually have muscles—lots of them.

The average male action figure has so much muscle that if he were a real man, he would have a 55-inch chest and a 27-inch bicep. This means that his bicep would be bigger than his waist. The poor guy would be so top heavy that he wouldn't be able to lean or bend down without falling on his head.[1]

The disturbing thing about these dolls and action figures is that they give children—even little children—the message that if they want to be powerful, important, beautiful and well-loved, they have to look like that character. The result is that teens today have no respect for their bodies. In fact, many abuse their bodies through starvation, cutting, drugging and drinking until they can no longer feel the pain of failure. Others neglect their bodies and see themselves as useless.

We must continually seek to help our teens understand the difference between what is truth and what is fiction, and in order for our young people to understand the difference, we must believe it and practice it ourselves. When you look at yourself in the mirror, what do you see? God sees His child whom He loves unconditionally. He loves you so much that He sent His only Son to die for you rather than be without you. As you come to really understand this for yourself, you will be able to communicate it to your group members. Always remember that in God's eyes, you and your teens are His masterpieces!

> *To say that I am made in the image of God is to say that love is the reason for my existence, for God is love.*
> THOMAS À KEMPIS

Note
1. "More than Just Dolls?" Body Image, http://www.johnriviello.com/bodyimage/dolls.html. Mattel, the makers of the Barbie Doll, sued The Body Shop for the advertisement.

group study guide

the stress of
negative self-image

starter

DESCRIBE YOURSELF: Ask the group members to pair up with a friend of the same gender. Then have them complete the following information.

Describe your height (short, tall, average): _____
Describe how you view your weight: _____
Describe your nose: _____
Describe your hair: _____
Describe your feet: _____
Describe your eyes: _____
Describe your mouth: _____

Note: You can download this group study guide in 8$^1/_2$" x 11" format at **www.gospellight.com/uncommon/dealing_with_stress_and_crisis.zip.**

Now complete the following information for your friend:

Describe your friend's height (short, tall, average): _____

Describe your friend's weight: _____

Describe your friend's nose: _____

Describe your friend's hair: _____

Describe your friend's feet: _____

Describe your friend's eyes: _____

Describe your friend's mouth: _____

When you are finished, compare your answers with your partner's. Then, as a large group, discuss the following questions:

1. Were the descriptions that you wrote about yourself and your friend's descriptions about you the same or different?
2. How accurately do you think your friend described you?
3. Were you honest when you described your friend?
4. What do you like the best about your physical appearance?
5. Was it hard or easy to share what you liked about yourself?
6. Would you change your appearance if you could?

message

The classic tale *Les Miserables* by Victor Hugo tells the story of a man named Jean Valjean. The story takes place during a dark time in France's history when people were starving and had no way to feed their families. Jean was one such man, and he stole food to feed his family. He was caught and sent to prison. After serving his time, he was released and wandered through the countryside, looking for a way to make money.

One day, Jean came to the house of a kind priest. The priest fed him and allowed him to spend the night. During the night, Jean stole the priest's silver knives, forks and spoons and, once again, was caught by the police as he made his escape. When the police saw the silver, they knew to whom it belonged, so they brought Jean back in chains to the priest. Jean knew he had stolen from a man who had been kind to him and he was sure the priest would press charges. Jean would be sent back to prison.

However, when the police asked the priest if Jean had stolen the silver, the priest said that he had not only given Jean the silverware, but that he had forgotten to take the silver candlesticks as well. The police had no alternative but to release Jean and leave. As the priest put the two candlesticks into Jean's hands, he said:

> My brother, you no longer belong to evil, but to good. It is your soul I am buying for you. I withdraw it from dark thoughts and the spirit of perdition, and I give it to God![1]

What the priest showed Jean was a picture of who Jesus is to us. No matter what we do, Jesus loves us. In fact, He loves us so much that He gave everything to give us the opportunity to know Him and belong to Him. Jesus poured out His love and compassion on us by dying to pay the price for our sins—something we all need but don't deserve.

our bodies are temples

In Romans 5:8, Paul says, "But God demonstrates his own love for us in this: While we were still sinners, Christ died for us." When we give our lives to Jesus, we belong to Him and know Him personally. We become a holy place for His Spirit to live. In 1 Corinthians 6:19-20, Paul describes this transaction this way:

Do you not know that your body is a temple of the Holy Spirit, who is in you, whom you have received from God? You are not your own; you were bought at a price. Therefore honor God with your body.

1. What is the purpose of a temple?

2. Who do these verses describe as a temple?

3. What price did God pay to allow us to belong to Him?

4. If we are Christians, how should treat our bodies?

we are valuable to God

Consider this fact: we are so valuable to God that He chose to sacrifice the life of His only Son so we could be set free from sin and live with Him forever. In John 3:16-17, Jesus describes God's love and purpose in a nutshell:

> *For God so loved the world that he gave his one and only Son, that whoever believes in him shall not perish but have eternal life. For God did not send his Son into the world to condemn the world, but to save the world through him.*

God created us, and He wants to be near us. Yet the relationship came at a price. It was expensive for Him to make a way to be with us, but He thinks that we are totally worth it! In Psalm 139:13-16, David writes:

> *For you created my inmost being;*
>   *you knit me together in my mother's womb.*
> *I praise you because I am fearfully and wonderfully made;*
>   *your works are wonderful,*
>   *I know that full well.*
> *My frame was not hidden from you*
>   *when I was made in the secret place.*
> *When I was woven together in the depths of the earth,*
>   *your eyes saw my unformed body.*
> *All the days ordained for me*
>   *were written in your book*
>   *before one of them came to be.*

1. God was there at the very beginning of us. Fill in the blanks based on this passage:

   He _____ our inmost being

   He _____ us together in our mother's womb

We are _____ and _____ made
All the _____ we will live are written, or known by God
before we have lived any of them.

2. What does God know about us?

    _____
    _____
    _____
    _____

3. What do the words "fearfully" and "wonderfully" say about
    how God looks at us?

    _____
    _____
    _____
    _____

4. What does the phrase, "All the days ordained for me were
    written in your book before one of them came to be," mean?

    _____
    _____
    _____
    _____

5. According to this psalm, what was God's intention in creat-
    ing you?

    _____
    _____
    _____
    _____

dig

Once we understand what God did for us and how He feels about us, we have a choice to make. We can choose to accept His gift and His love, or we can choose to reject it. If we accept His love—and accept Jesus' sacrifice for our sins—we are also accepting a new way of seeing ourselves.

1. What do the following sentences say about how you should see yourself and the person you truly are in God's eyes?

    You are a temple of the Holy Spirit.

    _____

    _____

    _____

    God's spirit lives within you.

    _____

    _____

    _____

    You belong to God.

    _____

    _____

    _____

    You have been saved from sin.

    _____

    _____

    _____

You have been given eternal life.

_____

_____

_____

_____

God created you, and all His works are wonderful.

_____

_____

_____

_____

God knows your future.

_____

_____

_____

_____

2. In 1 John 3:1, we read, "How great is the love the Father has lavished on us, that we should be called children of God! And that is what we are!" How does a loving father feel about his child?

_____

_____

_____

_____

3. What place does a loved child have in a household?

_____

_____

_____

_____

4. How does a child whose father generously lavishes him or her
    with love often feel about himself or herself?

    _____

    _____

    _____

5. What does it mean to you to be called a "child of God"?

    _____

    _____

    _____

apply

Read the following story about Anne, and then consider the difference between the way she sees herself and the way God sees her.

> Anne is obsessed about being thin. She deliberately starves
> herself and has developed an eating disorder known as
> anorexia nervosa, which literally means "loss of appetite
> because of nerves." Because she is not in the later stages,
> Anne feels hungry, but she chooses not to eat. She is ex-
> tremely thin, but when she looks in the mirror, she still
> sees herself as fat. So she exercises—a lot—and hides the
> fact that she uses products to "help keep her weight down."
> Anne is a perfectionist. If she doesn't get help and put on
> some weight, her obsession to be thin could be fatal.

How does Anne see herself? What are the consequences of her
negative self-image?

_____

_____

_____

an incredible creation

The following true or false quiz will give you a picture of just how incredible you are as a part of God's creation—worthy of loving care and protection. (Answers are given at the bottom of the page.)[2]

1. An unborn baby's heart doesn't start to beat until three months after conception.
2. Usually, the first hair that an unborn baby starts to grow is an eyebrow.
3. Thirteen weeks after conception, the unborn baby is the size of a watermelon, and its heart is the only organ that functions at this time.
4. Your brain is more complex than the most powerful computer.
5. Messages from your brain travel through your body at speeds of 100 miles per hour.
6. The average adult male is made up of 100 billion cells.
7. Twins have the same body odor.
8. Your body produces a chemical known as adrenaline that gives you super strength.
9. The human nose can identify 100 different smells.
10. Your eyes can distinguish up to one million color surfaces.
11. Your body contains enough water to fill a five-gallon tank.
12. Your feet can produce a pint of sweat a day.
13. Your stomach acid is strong enough to dissolve zinc.
14. Your bicep is the strongest muscle in the body.
15. A sneeze can travel at speeds in excess of 100 MPH.

Answers: (1) F—it starts beating about three weeks after conception; (2) T; (3) F—all of the baby's major organs are formed and fully functioning at 13 weeks; (4) T; (5) F—they travel at around 250 miles per hour; (6) F—adult males are made up of 100 trillion cells; (7) T; (8) T; (9) F—the human nose can identify 50,000 different smells; (10) T; (11) F—it can fill a 10-gallon tank; (12) T; (13) T; (14) F—your tongue is the strongest muscle in your body; (15) T.

holy and sacred

Unfortunately, many young people today do not realize just how incredible they are and do not see their bodies as being something holy or sacred. In fact, researchers report that 1 in every 5 teens has purposely injured themselves at some time (by cutting, scratching, burning, mutilating or hitting oneself, or anything else that causes bodily harm).[3] Even if a person does not carry self-abuse to this extreme, many abuse their bodies with smoking, drugs, alcohol and sex. But God wants so much more for us. In 1 Peter 2:9, we are told, "You are a chosen people, a royal priesthood, a holy nation, a people belonging to God, that you may declare the praises of him who called you out of darkness into his wonderful light."

1. Why do you think teens often have a difficult time seeing themselves as valuable?

2. Why do you think they participate in harmful activities?

3. What thoughts or feelings have you or someone you know expressed that indicate a negative self-image?

4. What events might have contributed to these feelings?

_____

_____

_____

5. What do you think God would say to you about your value? How would that make you feel?

_____

_____

_____

6. The Bible is God's Word, and the descriptions of God's love are intended for you personally. Review John 3:16-17 and 1 Peter 2:9. How would believing the truth of these words and living according to these truths change the way you see yourself?

_____

_____

_____

7. How would this change the way you behave or treat yourself?

_____

_____

_____

8. How can seeing yourself and others from God's point of view affect the way you respond to someone else who has an unhealthy self-image?

_____

_____

_____

reflect

1. On a scale of 1 to 10, how would you rate the degree to which you care about yourself?

1	2	3	4	5	6	7	8	9	10

    hate myself   love myself

2. What attitudes and behaviors do you display that show how you feel about yourself?

    _____

    _____

    _____

3. Is there anything you need to do right now to protect yourself from harm? If so, who can you talk to about it?

    _____

    _____

    _____

4. What would you have to change for your body (including your mind) to be a temple of the Holy Spirit?

    _____

    _____

    _____

5. What does a healthy self-image look like? How is it different from projecting yourself as being better than others?

    _____

    _____

    _____

6. How can you begin a relationship with God or strengthen your relationship with Him? Who can come alongside you to offer support and guidance?

_____

_____

_____

_____

_____

You are extremely valuable to God, as He proved through Jesus' sacrifice on the cross. So take time now to talk to God. Ask Him to help you change unhealthy things in your life, and then praise Him for His love and acceptance. Celebrate any progress He helps you to make in seeing yourself through His eyes!

meditation

For we are God's masterpiece. He has created us anew in Christ Jesus, so we can do the good things he planned for us long ago.

EPHESIANS 2:10, *NLT*

Notes

1. Victor Hugo, *Les Miserables* (Ware, UK: Wordsworth Editions, 1994), p. 73.
2. Information taken from "14 Facts About Your Unborn Baby," Ask a Mum, http://www.aska mum.co.uk/Pregnancy/Search-Results/Health/14-facts-about-your-unborn-baby/; "50 Incredibly Weird Facts About the Human Body," BSN Program, February 22, 2010, http://bsnprogram.com/2010/50-incredibly-weird-facts-about-the-human-body/; "Amazing Human Facts," Hub Pages, http://vinodpaulson.hubpages.com/hub/AMAZING_HUMAN_FACTS.
3. Jennifer LeClaire, "#CutForBieber Trend Mocks Pain of Tormented Teens" *Charisma News*, January 8, 2013, data from CNN poll. http://www.charismanews.com/opinion/35159-cut forbieber-trend-mocks-pain-of-tormented-teens.

unit II
dealing with crisis

Let's be perfectly honest: This is not going to be an easy unit for you or your group members. Any way you look at it, the traumatic events we are going to discuss can be extremely painful. However, though they are not easy subjects, perhaps we in the Church have dodged them for too long.

We must understand that kids need to be able to talk about the things they are going through, even if we don't feel completely comfortable with the subject matter—and there is no better place for them to talk through these issues than in the love and security of their churches or Bible study group. So don't be afraid to bring up difficult and traumatic issues from a Christian perspective, because if you don't, someone else will be glad to do so from a much more secular point of view.

In all four sessions in this unit, you will be given many opportunities for discussion with your group. Please don't forget that kids learn best when they talk, not when *you* talk. If you see your role as being a coach and guide to help your students discover answers for themselves, then you are being an effective teacher.

These sessions will do two things for your group. First, they will open the door to talk about negative and traumatic issues. Second, they will provide opportunities for you to present hope to your students. So remember this and remind your precious students that there is absolutely nothing too difficult for God to handle.

Here is one last suggestion. As you wade into what can be treacherous issues, don't be afraid to find resources and people who can come alongside you for encouragement, knowledge and counsel. There are many organizations whose mission is to serve people like you who are "difference makers" in the lives of young people and their families. Thanks for caring for kids.

the crisis of
sexual abuse

He heals the brokenhearted and binds up their wounds.

PSALM 147:3

What is sexual abuse? The standard definition is that sexual assault occurs when a male or female is tricked, coerced, seduced, intimidated, manipulated or forced in engaging in sexual activity with another person.[1] Sexual abuse can be one of the most painful and crippling things a teenager ever experiences. Even worse is the fact that the effects of the abuse can damage that teenager's life in many ways for years to come.

The reality of the effects can be seen in the story of two brothers named Justin and Matthiew. Justin, age 9, and Matthiew, age 11, attended a summer camp where a man named Peter was a counselor. Peter befriended the brothers, and later the whole family. Soon he was in and out of the family's home. The boys loved him, and their parents completely trusted him as a safe adult.

They even trusted Peter to the extent that they often allowed the boys to spend the night at his home.

One night, Peter began to sexually abuse the boys. When the boys questioned his actions, he told them that he loved them and that this was how people showed each other love. This went on for three years. Later, Peter accepted a job tutoring boys in England, which gave Matthiew the courage to tell his parents about the abuse. The parents contacted the police. Peter received a suspended three-year sentence with probation. But the nightmare was not over.

Peter continued to stalk the boys. He would tell them that they would never be able to have normal relationships—that they would be child molesters themselves. Both boys feared Peter's lie might be true. Matthiew tried to commit suicide twice, but failed. Several years later, Justin found the body of his father. He had committed suicide over the guilt he felt of being unable to protect his sons. Less than three months later, Justin successfully committed suicide. That same year, Matthiew also killed himself.[2]

This story seems almost too hard to believe, but it is true. Victims of sexual abuse need to know that there is help and healing in Jesus Christ. They need to know there are adults like you who care. Your compassion and unconditional love can help heal the unsightly scars of sexual abuse. You can be God's agent for help and freedom in Jesus Christ.

Out of suffering have emerged the strongest souls;
the most massive characters are sheared with scars.

E. H. CHAPIN

Notes

1. Definition from Dictionary.com, "sexual abuse." http://dictionary.reference.com/browse/sexual+abuse

2. "Think It Cannot Happen to You, to Your Child? Think Again," American Intelligence for Truth and Justice. http://www.myguardianprotection.com/sexual-predators.

the crisis of
sexual abuse

starter

RAPE QUESTIONS AND ANSWERS: Distribute copies of the "Questions About Sexual Abuse" quiz found at **www.gospellight.com/ uncommon/dealing_with_stress_and_crisis.zip.** Ask the group members to complete it to see what they understand about sexual abuse and, specifically, rape.

message

How does God feel about sexual abuse? Why does it happen? Is there hope for healing from such a trauma? These are vital questions that need to be answered in order to confront sexual abuse in a way that allows healing rather than pain and destruction.

Note: You can download this group study guide in 8¹/₂" x 11" format at **www.gospellight.com/uncommon/dealing_with_stress_and_crisis.zip.**

an amazing purpose

To do this, we first need to recognize that God created sex for an amazing purpose—to allow a husband and wife to express total trust and belonging to each other and to create children through this healthy and beautiful relationship. We are all created with the ability to experience this if we follow God's plan for sex. Genesis 2:23-25 describes the relationship between Adam and Eve, the first marriage God orchestrated:

> *The man said, "This is now bone of my bones and flesh of my flesh; she shall be called 'woman,' for she was taken out of man." For this reason a man will leave his father and mother and be united to his wife, and they will become one flesh. The man and his wife were both naked, and they felt no shame.*

1. How did the man feel about the woman?

    _____

    _____

    _____

2. What words describe the degree to which they belonged to each other?

    _____

    _____

    _____

3. What does their lack of shame say about the trust they had in each other?

    _____

    _____

    _____

sin and sexual perversion

Sex is supposed to be an expression of the bond of love a husband and wife have for each other. Sexual abuse takes something beautiful God created and twists it into something dark and unhealthy: sin. God has strong words to say about sexual sin because He knows the damage that comes from destroying trust and taking advantage of a person's vulnerability. Read the following verses and consider what they say about how God feels about sexual sin. Note that God's judgment is against those who refuse to follow His laws or leave their sin behind and seek His forgiveness.

The body is not meant for sexual immorality, but for the Lord, and the Lord for the body (1 Corinthians 6:13).

1. Whose design for how our bodies are treated should be followed? What is the opposite of sexual immorality?

[If] a man happens to meet a girl pledged to be married and rapes her, only the man who has done this shall die. Do nothing to the girl; she has committed no sin deserving death. . . . There was no one to rescue her (Deuteronomy 22:25-27).

2. Who is guilty in the event of a rape? To what is the crime of rape compared in this passage?

Do not be deceived: Neither the sexually immoral nor idolaters nor adulterers nor male prostitutes nor homosexual offenders nor thieves nor the greedy nor drunkards nor slanderers nor swindlers will inherit the kingdom of God (1 Corinthians 6:9-10).

3. What is the consequence for the sinners listed in these verses?

    _____

    _____

    _____

Note that the people listed in these verses are those who intentionally pursue sin, refuse to turn from it, and do not belong to Jesus Christ. It does not include those who have received God's forgiveness and strive to obey Him.

Marriage should be honored by all, and the marriage bed kept pure, for God will judge the adulterer and all the sexually immoral (Hebrews 13:4).

4. What does God say He will do to those who don't repent of their sexual sin?

    _____

    _____

    _____

Just as sin entered the world through one man, and death through sin, and in this way death came to all men, because all sinned. . . . For if, by the trespass of the one man, death reigned through that one man, how much more will those who receive God's abundant provision of grace and of the gift of righteousness reign in life through the one man, Jesus Christ (Romans 5:12,17).

5. Victims of abuse of any kind are not responsible for the actions of those who hurt them. Bad things happen when we don't deserve them; it's a fact of life. Why? According to these verses in Romans, who is responsible for the sin in our world?

_____

_____

_____

6. Who is the solution to sin in the world?

_____

_____

_____

And surely I am with you always, to the very end of the age (Matthew 28:20).

In this world you will have trouble. But take heart! I have overcome the world (John 16:33).

7. There is a tension on earth between sin and salvation. What promise of hope does Jesus make to those who belong to Him?

_____

_____

_____

dig

Victims of abuse often wonder why God didn't stop the abuse, or they question His ability and power to love and care for them. These are heartfelt questions—ones that need to be considered in order for the victim to heal from the trauma.

the freedom to choose

As Paul explains in Romans 5, God took a risk and gave us—humankind—the freedom to choose to obey Him and receive His strength to overcome sin. Many of the bad things we experience are a result of either our own choices or someone else's. They illustrate our need for a Savior and God's grace in giving us the opportunity to choose His love. In light of the verses you have studied, consider the following questions.

1. Why does God hate sexual abuse?

2. How does God feel about those who are abused?

3. What is the relationship between free choice and the existence of sin?

4. Why is free choice necessary for us to have a genuine relationship with God?

5. In what ways can God be with us during difficult times?

_____

_____

_____

6. What comfort can a victim of sexual abuse receive from a relationship with God?

_____

_____

_____

when choices lead to sin

Hagar was a slave in the household of Abraham and Sarah. God had promised that Abraham and Sarah would have a son, but they were getting up in years, so they intervened by having Hagar bear a child by Abraham. This was common practice in their day, but it was not part of God's plan. They sinned against God and Hagar.

Hagar became pregnant. Over time, the relationship between Sarah and Hagar grew tense. Sarah became abusive towards Hagar to the point that Hagar fled into the desert. God comforted her there and told her that she would name the baby Ishmael (which means "God hears") and that he would have many descendants. She responded to God by saying, "You are the God who sees me . . . I have now seen the One who sees me" (Genesis 16:13).

1. Hagar changed after this meeting. What two things show us that she truly met with the Lord?

   She named her son _____, which means _____ _____.
   She gave a name to the Lord: "You are the God who _____
   _____."

2. Hagar now understood that God saw her in her tough situation and had plans for her and Ishmael's future. How did this give her hope?

    _____

    _____

    _____

God's response to pain caused by another

The Bible tells us that Hagar returned to Abraham and Sarah. But, once again, Sarah mistreated her, and eventually Hagar and Ishmael were sent out into the desert with one container of water and some food. Ishmael was probably a teenager by this time. Hagar and her son ate the last of their food, and Ishmael drank the last drop of water from their container. Their situation became dire. Hagar and Ishmael gave up hope of survival. Yet God heard their cries, responded to their pain, and showed her a place where there was a well of water. "So she went and filled the skin with water and gave the boy a drink. God was with the boy as he grew up" (Genesis 21:19-20).

1. How does the story of Hagar show God's response to those who experience pain because of another person's sin?

    _____

    _____

    _____

2. What message of hope from God does this story give you? Where is God when you experience pain?

    _____

    _____

    _____

apply

God does hear us when we cry to Him for help. Sometimes, the help we receive doesn't always look the way we expect it to look. It can come in the form of a concerned parent, a caring teacher, a friend who confronts us, or even a police officer. Sometimes help comes right away, but sometimes we have to go out and grab the help that God is offering. If you or a person you know has been sexually abused, there are four important and life-transforming points you need to understand.

1. it's not your fault

Many people partly blame themselves for the sexual abuse that occurred to them, but it is important to recognize that sexual abuse is *always* the fault of the abuser.

1. Why do you think a person might blame himself or herself for the abuse?

   _____

   _____

   _____

2. Is that person believing the truth or a lie? Why?

   _____

   _____

   _____

3. Why is it healthy to realize abuse is solely the fault of the abuser?

   _____

   _____

   _____

2. you need to seek help

Most people who have been sexually abused are afraid to tell any-one about it. However, sexual abuse can lead to other problems the longer you wait, and it's hard to recover without help. Your pain won't go away by itself, so it is important to tell people who can do something about the wrong that has been done to you. Here are several things you need to do if someone has sexually abused you:

- Get to a safe place.
- Do not bathe or change clothes (this is to preserve the evidence of the crime).
- Call a rape or sexual abuse crisis hotline.
- Have a trusted friend or family member go with you to the hospital emergency room (take a change of clothes if possible) so that: (1) they can preserve the evidence, which is important if you decide to prosecute; (2) determine any injuries that you may have; and (3) check for sexually transmitted diseases and pregnancy.
- Report the crime to police.

Making a police report will benefit you directly in several ways:

- Reporting the assault is a way of regaining your sense of personal power and control.
- Reporting enables you to do something concrete about the crime committed against you.
- Reporting helps ensure that you receive the most immediate and comprehensive assistance available.

Making a police report will also help prevent other people from being raped. Most rapists are repeat offenders, so reporting and prosecuting the assailant are essential to the prevention of rape. Remember that if the rape is not reported, the assailant cannot be apprehended.

1. What kinds of problems could develop if a person who has suffered abuse keeps his or her pain locked inside? How could telling another person help?

_____

_____

_____

2. If you or someone you know has been abused, what changes in behavior and emotions have you noticed?

_____

_____

_____

3. If you ever experience abuse, who is one person you could go to for help who would listen to you, go with you to the hospital, and accompany you to the police station to make a report?

_____

_____

_____

Being persistent about getting help is important. Asking God for wisdom and help to find the right people will equip you to take this step.

3. there is hope

Millions of people have been abused, and many have sought help, worked through their pain, and are now living happy lives. One such group of survivors started an organization called The Clothesline Project (www.clotheslineproject.org). They believe that once a person is able to tell someone about his or her abuse, that person is no longer a victim.[1]

1. Why do you think telling someone about your sexual abuse can help you to no longer be a victim?

_____

_____

_____

2. How could sharing your experience help someone else?

_____

_____

_____

_____

3. How can listening to and supporting a person who has been abused make a difference in his or her life? How will it affect your life?

_____

_____

_____

4. God cares!

Frankly, most people who have experienced any kind of sexual abuse struggle in their relationship with God. Perhaps too many spend their energies blaming God instead of being comforted by Him. They need to recognize that He loves them and wants to heal their wounds. Read John 11:17-44. Although this story is about Jesus responding to the death of His friend Lazarus, there are numerous insights you can gain that relate to how God cares for someone who is hurting.

1. What was Jesus' reaction when he saw Mary weeping in verses 33-36?

    _____

    _____

    _____

2. Does this reaction surprise you? What does this tell you about Jesus?

    _____

    _____

    _____

3. What does Jesus do in verses 43-44?

    _____

    _____

    _____

4. Jesus has the power to heal anyone. He also deeply loves people and can feel their pain. How does knowing this help you to have hope, especially if you have been sexually abused?

    _____

    _____

    _____

    _____

If you or someone you know has been sexually abused, now is the time to seek the help you need to start the road to recovery. Seek help within the next 24 hours.

reflect

A person who commits sexual abuse against another person may trick, coerce, seduce, intimidate, manipulate or force that person into not offering any resistance to sexual activity. For this reason, it is important to clearly define and identify sexual abuse in order to protect yourself and get help if you or someone you know has been victimized. Sexual abuse can include activities such as:

- Showing children pornographic materials
- Taking nude pictures of another person
- An adult exposing his or her body to a child or asking the child to expose himself or herself
- Fondling private areas of another person's body
- Intimate kissing
- Genital contact
- Intercourse
- Rape—including date rape or acquaintance rape

1. Most victims of abuse know their abusers. Is there anyone in your life whom you feel puts you at risk of being sexually abused? Do you have any friends who may be at risk?

   _____

   _____

   _____

2. Have you or a friend ever faced the choice of reporting being sexually abused? If so, who did you tell? If not, why didn't you tell?

   _____

   _____

   _____

3. Did you have support from loving people during this experience, or were you able to give support to another? What kind of help would have been the most useful?

    _____

    _____

    _____

4. How would your faith in God be affected by a crisis such as sexual abuse?

    _____

    _____

    _____

5. How can a healthy relationship with God affect your ability to heal after experiencing a crisis such as sexual abuse?

    _____

    _____

    _____

6. Read Romans 8:38-39. Why can you be confident in God's love for you—even if you have been sexually abused?

    _____

    _____

    _____

7. What are some of the things Paul says cannot get between you and God's love?

    _____

    _____

    _____

    _____

8. What are some difficult situations that you are going through in your own life?

_____

_____

_____

9. On the left side of your list of hard situations, write your name. On the right side of the list, write the word "God." Now take a red marker and draw a cross through the list. Above the list, write the words:

NOTHING CAN SEPARATE ME
FROM GOD OR HIS LOVE!

How could this wonderful truth make a difference in the life of someone you know who has been abused?

_____

_____

_____

meditation

*Come to me, all you who are weary and burdened, and I will
give you rest. Take my yoke upon you and learn from me, for I
am gentle and humble in heart, and you will find rest for your souls.
For my yoke is easy and my burden is light.*

MATTHEW 11:28-30

Note
1. Jane Park, "Stories of Sexual Abuse Survivors on Display with Clothesline Project," MiNBC News, April 17, 2012. http://www.minbcnews.com/news/story.aspx?id=743157.

the crisis of suicide

Do you not know? Have you not heard? The LORD is the everlasting God, the Creator of the ends of the earth. He will not grow tired or weary, and his understanding no one can fathom. He gives strength to the weary and increases the power of the weak. Even youths grow tired and weary, and young men stumble and fall; but those who hope in the LORD will renew their strength. They will soar on wings like eagles; they will run and not grow weary, they will walk and not be faint.

ISAIAH 40:28-31

Suicide. What emotions fill you as you read this word? It's scary, sad, tragic and confusing. The reality is that people do commit suicide, and some of those are people who attend our churches.

There is a story about a young man named Phil who took more than 40 Advil pills in attempt to kill himself. Phil wasn't a high school student, nor was he in junior high. Phil was a college student and a volunteer junior-high leader in a local church.

When the youth pastor of the church, who was named Todd, arrived at the hospital, he found Phil connected to tubes that ran every which way. Black charcoal lined his mouth and nostrils. Monitors beeped and hummed. Every few minutes, Phil's body writhed and squirmed as he mumbled and groaned in agony.

Todd was troubled by questions for which he had no answers. Why would Phil attempt suicide? Hadn't anyone seen this coming? How had the entire church missed what was going on in Phil's life? In fact, Todd's experience is not an isolated one. Many churches have lost individuals to suicide. How can we prevent this from happening?

One of the most useful ways to keep suicide from catching you or your students off guard is by understanding the importance of suicide prevention. How many teenage suicide attempts could have been prevented if every teenager had someone with whom he or she could talk? You are in the unique position to help kids in crisis. You are standing in the gap for today's teenagers. You will probably never know how many tragedies have been averted by your presence in your teens' lives.

This session will give you the tools you need to understand the facts about suicide, how to help your group members talk about it, and how to clarify the many myths about it. Most important, it will give your young people an action plan for understanding and dealing with their own feelings of suicide and how to help their friends who are also in crisis. It will provide you with an opportunity to minister to those students on the verge of becoming the next Phil.

Life is a voyage. The winds of life come strong from every point;
yet each will speed thy course along, if thou with steady hand when tempests
blow canst keep thy course aright and never once let go.
THEODORE CHICKERING WILLIAMS

the crisis of suicide

starter

THE FACTS OF SUICIDE: Read the following to your group:

- Each year, approximately 149,000 youth between the ages of 10 and 24 receive medical care for self-inflicted injuries.
- Suicide is the third leading cause of death for youth between the ages of 10 and 24.
- Suicide results in approximately 4,400 teenage lives lost each year.
- 15 percent of all teenagers seriously consider suicide.
- 11 percent of all teenagers reported creating a plan for suicide.
- 7 percent of all teenagers reported trying to take their own life.[1]

Note: You can download this group study guide in 8½" x 11" format at **www.gospellight.com/uncommon/dealing_with_stress_and_crisis.zip.**

Now ask the group members to indicate which is most correct for their school:

- These statistics seem about right.
- These statistics seem to be higher than what I think actually happens.
- These statistics seem to be lower than what I think actually happens.

Have the students gather with a couple of friends or, as a large group, discuss whether they think the following statement is true: "Suicide is a permanent solution to a temporary problem."

message

There was a man in the Bible named Job who suffered greatly—beyond what most people would ever have happen in their lives. When faced with one crisis after another Job had a choice to make. In this section, we will see the attitude he took and how he approached all the losses he suffered.

disaster strikes

Job was a wealthy man who was known as the greatest among all the people of the East. He owned 7,000 sheep, 3,000 camels, 500 yoke of oxen and 500 donkeys. He had seven sons and three daughters and also had a large number of servants. But that was all soon to change:

One day when Job's sons and daughters were feasting and drinking wine at the oldest brother's house, a messenger came to Job and said, "The oxen were plowing and the donkeys were grazing nearby, and the Sabeans [an ancient tribe of people who lived in what is today

Yemen] attacked and carried them off. They put the servants to the sword, and I am the only one who has escaped to tell you!"

While he was still speaking, another messenger came and said, "The fire of God fell from the sky and burned up the sheep and the servants, and I am the only one who has escaped to tell you!"

While he was still speaking, another messenger came and said, "The Chaldeans [an ancient tribe of people who lived in what is today Iraq] formed three raiding parties and swept down on your camels and carried them off. They put the servants to the sword, and I am the only one who has escaped to tell you!"

While he was still speaking, yet another messenger came and said, "Your sons and daughters were feasting and drinking wine at the oldest brother's house, when suddenly a mighty wind swept in from the desert and struck the four corners of the house. It collapsed on them and they are dead, and I am the only one who has escaped to tell you!"

1. What was the first loss Job suffered in verses 13-15?

   ---

2. What happened to the sheep and the servants in verse 16?

   ---

3. What happened to the camels and the servants in verse 17?

   ---

4. The losses now come closer to home. How did Job lose his
    sons and daughters in verses 18-19?

    ....

    ....

    ....

the cause of the trouble

These losses weren't the end of Job's troubles. In Job 2:7, we read he
was afflicted with "painful sores from the soles of his feet to the
top of his head." The Bible also tells us the cause of Job's crises: Satan had challenged God, saying that the only reason Job loved and
obeyed Him was because he had an easy life filled will blessings.

> *"Does Job fear God for nothing?" Satan replied. "Have you not
> put a hedge around him and his household and everything he has?
> You have blessed the work of his hands, so that his flocks and herds
> are spread throughout the land. But stretch out your hand and
> strike everything he has, and he will surely curse you to your face"*
> (Job 1:9-11).

God didn't strike Job with these difficult losses, but He did allow Satan to do so—though He did not allow Satan's to take Job's
life (see Job 2:1-6). This was not because Job did anything wrong.
In fact, in Job 1:8, God tells Satan, "Have you considered my ser-
vant Job? There is no one on earth like him; he is blameless and
upright, a man who fears God and shuns evil."

Have you ever heard the saying, "Bad things happen to good
people?" From our perspective, this doesn't seem to make sense.
We often associate being good with being rewarded with good
things—not with tests of our faith or hardships that are beyond
our comprehension. Yet this is exactly what was happening to Job.

1. What was it about Job—a good man who was doing all the right things in God's eyes—that made him a target for Satan's attacks?

----

2. Why do you think God allowed Satan to conduct these attacks? What was being tested in Job's life?

Job's reaction to his losses

When hit with this disaster, Job expressed his grief and suffering openly to the Lord (see Job 3:1-26). He questioned why God was letting these things happen—saying, "I despise my life"—and asked God to end his suffering (see 7:16). His wife told him to curse God and die (see 2:9), and his friends told him his suffering must have come from something he did wrong (see 4:7-8). Job was in pain and surrounded by negative input from the people in his life. Still, he bared his soul to God and proclaimed his innocence, not holding back the depths of his despair. Look at his response:

> At this [hearing about the loss of his possessions and children], Job got up and tore his robe and shaved his head. Then he fell to the ground in worship and said: "Naked I came from my mother's womb, and naked I will depart. The LORD gave and the LORD has taken away; may the name of the LORD be praised." In all this, Job did not sin by charging God with wrongdoing (Job 1:20-22).

After declaring his innocence to his friends and questioning why God had let these things happen, God answered Job. Eventually, Job said to God:

> *I am unworthy—how can I reply to you? I put my hand over my mouth. I spoke once, but I have no answer—twice, but I will say no more. . . . I know that you can do all things; no plan of yours can be thwarted. You asked, "Who is this that obscures my counsel without knowledge?" Surely I spoke of things I did not understand, things too wonderful for me to know (Job 40:4-5; 42:2-3).*

1. How did Job respond to the loss of his possessions and children (see Job 1:20-22)?

   _____

   _____

   _____

   _____

   _____

2. Who did Job acknowledge as in charge of the course of his life—which includes the timing of his death?

   _____

   _____

   _____

3. What does Job's response say about his relationship to God?

   _____

   _____

   _____

   _____

God's response and restoration

God doesn't answer each of Job's specific questions about why he is enduring such hardship. Instead, God asks Job a series of questions. Read a sample of these questions from Job 38 and fill in the blanks:

- Where were you when I _____ the _____ _____ (verse 4)?
- Who ____ ___ the _____ behind doors (verse 8)?
- What is the way to the place where the _____ is dispersed, or the place where the _____ _____ are scattered over the earth (verse 24)?
- Can you bring forth the _____ in their seasons (verse 32)?
- Do you send the _____ _____ on their way? Do they report to you, "Here we are" (verse 35)?
- Do you _____ the prey for the _____ (verse 39)?

Job's conversation with God reassured him that God understood his circumstances and had authority over them. In Job 42:12-17, we read how God responded to Job's faithfulness and humility:

The LORD blessed the latter part of Job's life more than the former part. He had fourteen thousand sheep, six thousand camels, a thousand yoke of oxen and a thousand donkeys. And he also had seven sons and three daughters. The first daughter he named Jemimah, the second Keziah and the third Keren-Happuch. Nowhere in all the land were there found women as beautiful as Job's daughters, and their father granted them an inheritance along with their brothers. After this, Job lived a hundred and forty years; he saw his children and their children to the fourth generation. And so he died, old and full of years.

What was the result of Job's perseverance through extreme hardship?

_____

_____

_____

dig

Stories of hardship and despair go beyond the facts of a person's circumstances—they involve the person's emotions, character and relationship with God.

1. What was God really asking Job through His questions—or telling Job about Himself?

   _____

   _____

   _____

   _____

2. Aside from the material rewards Job enjoyed after his time of testing, how would you describe the quality of his life?

   _____

   _____

   _____

3. What would have happened if Job had decided to kill himself to end all of the trouble he was having? (Remember, he often wished he would die and end his misery; see Job 7:16.)

   _____

   _____

   _____

4. How would suicide have been a permanent solution to a tem-
    porary—though long and difficult—circumstance for Job?

    _____

    _____

    _____

5. Why do you think it was difficult for Job to find hope when
    he was overwhelmed by his despair?

    _____

    _____

    _____

6. How did seeking God help Job? How did God's answer com-
    fort him?

    _____

    _____

    _____

Our relationship with God is just that: a relationship. It goes
beyond asking for help and waiting for a response. No one wants
to endure what Job did, but Job came through it knowing the
God he had obeyed and worshiped personally. God didn't cause
his difficulty, but He limited it and used it to allow Job to really
know Him.

apply

Suicide has cut short the lives of many who were blessed with
great talent. Many people who saw no way out of difficulties made
the choice to end their lives and the possibility of a future in
which hope could be restored. Consider the following story.

the effects of suicide on others

The rock world was shaken by the suicide of one of its most gifted artists of the 1990s, Kurt Cobain of the rock group Nirvana. In life, Cobain was often in pain. His songs often told of the void in his heart, and the rock world knew of his self-destructive streak. He had been addicted to heroin, and days before his death in Seattle, Washington, he had fled a drug rehabilitation center. Cobain, like many mega rock stars before him, decided life was not worth living.

What Cobain didn't know was how his suicide would affect someone very close to him, his daughter, Francis Bean Cobain. Both of Francis' parents, Kurt and his wife, Courtney Love, had struggled with drugs for years. When Francis was born, everyone assumed she would most likely be born addicted to the drugs her parents had taken. Fortunately, she was born healthy. However, two days after her birth, a social worker showed up at the hospital to investigate the alleged drug abuse of her parents, and her parents had to struggle to regain custody of her.

Francis was two years old when her father committed suicide. Her mother continued to take drugs, and when she was just eight years old, her mother overdosed on drugs in front of her. While the two waited for the ambulance, Francis made her mother a cup of tea.

Francis had at least one good thing in her life at this point: her grandmother. While nannies came and went in her parents' household, her grandmother was always there for her. As her mother lost and regained custody of her over and over again, her grandmother was there when she needed her. Eventually, her grandmother was granted temporary guardianship, and Francis was allowed to live with her. Her parents choices to abuse drugs and attempt suicide (successfully, by her dad) had a huge impact on everyone in their lives—especially Francis.

Today, Francis has beaten the odds. She has many hopes and dreams that she is setting out to fulfill. She is very much her own person. She has said, "I don't want to be titled as Courtney Love and Kurt Cobain's daughter. I want to be thought of as Frances Cobain." And she is.[2]

1. What circumstances contributed to Kurt Cobain's decision to commit suicide?

2. Who else was affected by Kurt's death? How were they affected?

3. Imagine you had five minutes to talk to Kurt Cobain. After what you have learned from Job and what you know about Kurt's daughter, what could you say to him?

important truths to understand

There are two important truths you need to know if you or someone near you has ever considered committing suicide.

First, *you have choices,* and it is important for you to consider the impact your choices will have on the people in your life. People who are considering suicide often think it is their *only* choice. Yet you can seek God and what He has for you—God *can* help you recognize that the hopelessness you are feeling right now is temporary (even though it hurts) and reach out for help. Consider the difference a relationship with God could have made in the life of someone like Kurt Cobain.

Second, *you do not know what the future holds.* You cannot predict what is going to happen or see the whole picture—but God can. You could be one step away from your whole life taking a turn in a better direction. So never give up.

1. In 1 Corinthians 2:9, Paul says, "No eye has seen, no ear has heard, no mind has conceived what God has prepared for those who love him." What can God see that we cannot see?

   _____

   _____

   _____

2. What hope do you see in Paul's words? Why?

   _____

   _____

   _____

3. What factors can contribute to feelings of hopelessness?

   _____

   _____

   _____

4. Why do teens sometimes consider suicide as a solution to their problems?

   _____

   _____

   _____

it's friday, but sunday's coming

Tony Campolo often tells a story of a great African-American pastor, S. M. Lockridge, who preached a simple message to his congregation: "Its Friday, but Sunday's Coming."[3] The theme, of course, was taken from Jesus' death (on Friday) and resurrection (on Sunday). The death and resurrection of Christ is a cornerstone of hope. Friday represents the negative issues—sin, disease, broken relationships, depression, anger, pain and hopelessness. Sunday represents the restoration—hope, victory over sin, new life, new blessings, forgiveness, freedom, peace and joy.

1. Take a few moments to write down your problems under "Friday" and the hopeful solutions under "Sunday."

    Friday (Problems)   Sunday (Hopeful Solutions)

    _____   _____
    _____   _____
    _____   _____
    _____   _____

2. In Deuteronomy 31:8, Moses says, "The LORD himself goes before you and will be with you; he will never leave you nor forsake you. Do not be afraid; do not be discouraged." How can this promise from God make a difference in your life when you feel hopeless?

    _____
    _____
    _____

3. Even if you aren't feeling down right now, the changes are that one day you will need to hang on to hope. Who are at

least three people in your life to whom you can turn when you need hope?

_____

_____

_____

4. Who can you give hope to this next week? What specifically can you do to offer them hope?

_____

_____

_____

reflect

Take a few minutes to reflect on where you stand on the issue of suicide. On what is your point of view based? Look at the facts below and consider what you have studied from God's Word. Then, if you or someone you know is feeling hopeless and at risk, plan steps you can take to get help and support.

1. At the beginning of this session we looked at a few statistics about suicide. Here are a few more items to consider. For each statement, indicate whether you believe it to be true or false. (See the answers on page 113.)

	T	F
1. People who talk about suicide won't do it.	☐	☐
2. Mentioning suicide to a friend in crisis can help that person.	☐	☐
3. All suicidal people are mentally ill.	☐	☐
4. There are usually warning signs before a suicide.	☐	☐

                                                              T   F

5. When the depression lifts, the suicide crisis is over. ☐ ☐

6. Suicidal people often seek medical help.   ☐ ☐

2. What are some of the things you have learned about suicide in this session?

_____

_____

_____

3. Think about a difficult situation you are facing. What are your feelings about it?

_____

_____

_____

4. Spend some time in prayer. How do you feel God wants you to respond in this situation (what choices and changes can you make)?

_____

_____

_____

(1) F—80 percent of suicide victims talked about it, but friends and family didn't take them seriously; (2) T—Talking about suicide can help the friend see what others think about it and the impact it has on others; (3) F—Only a small percentage of those who commit suicide are diagnosed as mentally ill; (4) T—Warning signs include withdrawal, giving away prized possessions, a difficult romantic breakup, and heavy use of drugs and alcohol; (5) F—the abrupt lifting of depression often suggests the suicidal person has finally decided to end his or her life; (6) T—Strangely enough, three out of four people who attempt suicide usually seek medical help in the last three months of their lives.

5. When you feel hopeless, how can you trust in God's promise to be with always?

_____

_____

_____

_____

6. Now spend time in prayer for a friend whom you know is struggling with hopelessness. What do you feel God wants you to do to help that friend?

_____

_____

_____

_____

meditation

He will take pity on the weak and the needy and save the needy
from death. He will rescue them from oppression and violence,
for precious is their blood in his sight.

PSALM 72:13-14

Notes

1. "Suicide Prevention: Youth Suicide," Centers for Disease Control and Prevention. http://www.cdc.gov/violenceprevention/pub/youth_suicide.html.
2. Story adapted from "Frances Bean Cobain," Biography.com. http://www.biography.com/people/frances-bean-cobain-281996.
3. A video of this story can be seen at http://www.youtube.com/watch?v=UcbKWT10z34. Another dramatic version can be found at http://www.youtube.com/watch?v=Tn94B3GHcjY).

the crisis of
HIV/AIDS

Even though I walk through the valley of the shadow of death, I will fear no evil,
for you are with me; your rod and your staff, they comfort me.

PSALM 23:4

AIDS (Acquired Immune Deficiency Syndrome) has been a death sentence for many people. It has spread all over the world through a virus known as HIV (Human Immunodeficiency Virus). There are countries today that are literally being destroyed by this disease. In 2009, 1.8 million people died due to HIV/AIDS, and 1.3 million of these deaths occurred in Africa. In South Africa, 1 in 5 adults is HIV positive, and there are between 180,000 to 280,000 children infected with the disease.[1]

Your students are being fed information by our culture on using condoms as a so-called "safe sex" measure and are being barraged by a wealth of misinformation about sexually transmitted diseases, including HIV and AIDS. We need to supply our students with the truth. If we want to protect them from the ravages of sexually transmitted diseases, we need challenge them with God's call for sexual abstinence before marriage.

AIDS and other sexually transmitted diseases are weak motivators for sexual purity, as most teenagers don't feel they are at risk. You can give them a higher reason for remaining sexually pure. You have the awesome privilege and opportunity of presenting to your students God's plan for living a holy and pleasing life. Their choices can literally be a matter of life and death.

You also have the opportunity to teach your students how to respond to those who are suffering through the AIDS crisis with the compassion of Jesus Christ, who "is patient with you, not wanting anyone to perish, but everyone to come to repentance" (2 Peter 3:9). The message of Jesus is one of truth, comfort, hope and eternal life—and it is for everyone.

I'm scared to die such a young man. I'd like a little more time.
I lived in the fast lane. If only God will give me a break.
28-YEAR-OLD VICTIM OF AIDS

Note

1. "11 Facts About HIV in Africa," DoSomething.org. http://www.dosomething.org/actnow/tips andtools/11-facts-about-hiv-africa.

the crisis of
HIV/AIDS

starter

HIV RISK FACTORS: Have your group members write "agree," "disagree" or "not sure" next to each of the statements below.[1]

1. Young people who experiment with cigarettes, alcohol, sex and drugs could be in danger of being infected with HIV (Human Immunodeficiency Virus). _____

2. A child who tries a cigarette in the fourth or fifth grade will likely try riskier behavior later. _____

3. Girls who develop physically at an early age could be more at risk because they may unwittingly attract older males

and lack the maturity or social skills to protect themselves from unwelcome advances. _____

4. Adolescents who have serious problems in school are at
   risk because they possibly lack self-esteem and are likely
   to be tempted by drugs, alcohol or sex in order to feel good
   about themselves. _____

5. Impoverished teens in inner cities are in a special risk category because, more than likely, drug activity takes place
   in their neighborhoods and there is far more pressure to
   use drugs and have sex at an early age. _____

Ask the group members to discuss their answers with a few friends.
Note that all of the answers are *true*. These are each referred to as
"gateway factors" because they often lead to more serious problems, including exposure to HIV and other STDs (sexually transmitted diseases). Next, make copies of the following list (also found
at **www.gospellight.com/uncommon/dealing_with_stress_
and_crisis.zip**), which gives several facts about HIV/AIDS and some
of the specific ways it can be contracted. (Note that this is not a
complete list, but it will give you the basics).

- People who have HIV may appear and feel healthy for
  years. Unless they have been tested every three months
  after exposure, they will not know if they are infected and
  can infect others.

- There is no cure for HIV, just treatments that improve the
  health of a person with HIV and slow the progression of
  the virus into AIDS (Acquired Immune Deficiency Syndrome). These treatments are daily, lifelong and come at a
  financial and physical cost.

- AIDS is the late stage of HIV infection and occurs when a person's immune system is weak and unable to fight off disease.

- In a year, one person dies of AIDS for every 3 people newly diagnosed with HIV.

- HIV is spread primarily by having sex with someone who has HIV. Condoms lower the risk, but they do not guarantee protection.

- Having multiple sex partners greatly increases the possibility of contracting HIV (and numerous other STDs).

- Sharing needles or other equipment for injecting drugs increases the risk of contracting HIV. Tatooing or body piercing using non-sterile equipment also increases the risk.

- Less common (but possible) ways to contract the disease include contact between broken skin, wounds or mucous membranes with HIV-infected blood or blood-contaminated body fluids.

- HIV *cannot* be spread by insects or through air, water, saliva, tears, sweat, or casual contact (hand holding, closed-mouth kissing).[2]

STDs in general—including HIV—are present in 1 in 4 teens. There is no risk of STDs for those who are virgins (not sexually active). The risk of contracting HIV for virgins who are not drug users is also minimal. Those who are sexually active have a 50/50 chance of being infected with at least one STD, including HIV. Each risk factor that is present in a person's life greatly increases his or her odds of infection.[3]

message

It is critical to know the truth when it comes to dealing with issues such as HIV and AIDS, because having accurate information can mean the difference between *life and death*. Many people struggle with the definition of truth and make choices based on what they "feel" is true for them. However, the Bible tells us there is a standard for truth: truth that is absolute and unchanging. We can rely on this truth to guide our lives, protect us and allow us to encourage others who are hurting.

a look at truth

Let's examine a few passages from the Bible that speak about what truth is and how it benefits us.

> *Since you are my rock and my fortress, for the sake of your name lead and guide me. Free me from the trap that is set for me, for you are my refuge. Into your hands I commit my spirit; redeem me, O LORD, the God of truth* (Psalm 31:3-5).

1. What words does David, who wrote this psalm, use to describe who God is?

   _____

   _____

   _____

2. What words does he use to describe what God does for the one who seeks Him?

   _____

   _____

   _____

The Word became flesh and made his dwelling among us. We have seen his glory, the glory of the One and Only, who came from the Father, full of grace and truth (John 1:14).

3. How does John describe Jesus in this verse?

Jesus answered, "I am the way and the truth and the life. No one comes to the Father except through me" (John 14:6).

4. What does Jesus say about Himself in this verse? What does He mean when He says that no one comes to the Father except through Him?

----

the impact of truth

Truth is more than a fact; it is the person of Jesus Christ. One of the most common phrases Jesus used when He was teaching was, "I tell you the truth" (see, for example, Matthew 5:18,26; 6:2,5,16; 8:10; 10:15,23,42). We have access to genuine truth through our relationship with Jesus and our access to His Word, the Bible. The following verses describe the impact this truth from God can have in our lives:

A truthful witness gives honest testimony, but a false witness tells lies. Reckless words pierce like a sword, but the tongue of the wise brings healing (Proverbs 12:17-18).

A truthful witness saves lives, but a false witness is deceitful
(Proverbs 14:25).

Then you will know the truth, and the truth will set you free
(John 8:32).

They will turn their ears away from the truth and turn aside to
myths (2 Timothy 4:4).

1. What do these verses say are the result when people are truthful and rely on God's truth to guide them?

   _____

   _____

   _____

2. According to these verses, how can truthful words help people?

   _____

   _____

   _____

3. According to 2 Timothy 4:4, when someone turns away from the truth, on what is he or she relying?

   _____

   _____

   _____

the freedom of truth

HIV and AIDS have impacted individuals, families and cultures and have caused great suffering in our world. Accurate information—the truth—allows people to protect themselves physically, but it also frees them to reach out to those who are suffering. Jesus, who was the embodiment of truth, reached out to many who were suffering during His time on earth, including those who were oppressed by demons, social outcasts or were enduring physical pain—including highly infectious diseases like leprosy. The following are just a few examples that show His heart for the hurting.

While Jesus was having dinner at Levi's house, many tax collectors and "sinners" were eating with him and his disciples, for there were many who followed him. When the teachers of the law who were Pharisees saw him eating with the "sinners" and tax collectors, they asked his disciples: "Why does he eat with tax collectors and 'sinners'?" On hearing this, Jesus said to them, "It is not the healthy who need a doctor, but the sick. I have not come to call the righteous, but sinners" (Mark 2:15-17).

1. Who did Jesus seek out? Why?

   ----

2. Jesus' followers were with him at this "party." What do you think Jesus was modeling for those who follow Him?

A Canaanite woman from that vicinity came to him, crying out, "Lord, Son of David, have mercy on me! My daughter is suffering terribly from demon-possession." . . . Jesus answered, "Woman, you have great faith! Your request is granted." And her daughter was healed from that very hour (Matthew 15:21,28).

3. This woman was an "outcast" in the sense that she was a descendant of the ancient Canaanites, the biblical enemies of Israel who often led God's people into idolatry. How did Jesus show mercy on her in spite of this fact?

When she heard about Jesus, she came up behind him in the crowd and touched his cloak, because she thought, "If I just touch his clothes, I will be healed." Immediately her bleeding stopped and she felt in her body that she was freed from her suffering. At once Jesus realized that power had gone out from him. He turned around in the crowd and asked, "Who touched my clothes?" . . . Then the woman, knowing what had happened to her, came and fell at his feet and, trembling with fear, told him the whole truth. He said to her, "Daughter, your faith has healed you. Go in peace and be freed from your suffering" (Mark 5:27-30,33-34).

4. This woman had been suffering from bleeding for 12 years. How did Jesus express His compassion for her condition?

----

5. What did this woman and the Canaanite woman both have in common?

----

dig

Truth and compassion go hand in hand. In Ephesians 4:15, Paul says we are to speak "the truth in love," and in 1 John 3:17-18 we see how truth is expressed in the life of a follower of Christ through his or her actions:

> *If anyone has material possessions and sees his brother in need but has no pity on him, how can the love of God be in him? Dear children, let us not love with words or tongue but with actions and in truth.*

1. What is the difference between absolute truth and what a person believes to be true for his or situation? What is the basis for each one?

   _____

   _____

   _____

2. How does knowing the truth of God lead to acts of compassion for those who are suffering?

   _____

   _____

   _____

3. Why is it important to have an absolute standard for truth?

   _____

   _____

   _____

4. How does having God as your standard of truth affect how you make decisions?

5. HIV and AIDS are surrounded by misunderstanding, bad information and fear. Having truthful and accurate information about these diseases allows us to respond intelligently to this issue, show *compassion*, and have a positive impact on those affected. As we have seen, Jesus is our model for loving those who are hurting. What is the result of sharing truth without compassion—especially in a situation where sin may be involved?

6. How is presenting truth in love like presenting Jesus to a hurting person?

While Jesus was in one of the towns, a man came along who was covered with leprosy. When he saw Jesus, he fell with his face to the ground and begged him, "Lord, if you are willing, you can make me clean." Jesus reached out his hand and touched the man. "I am willing," he said. "Be clean!" And immediately the leprosy left him (Luke 5:12-13).

*Now on his way to Jerusalem, Jesus traveled along the border be-
tween Samaria and Galilee. As he was going into a village, ten
men who had leprosy met him. They stood at a distance and called
out in a loud voice, "Jesus, Master, have pity on us!" When he saw
them, he said, "Go, show yourselves to the priests." And as they
went, they were cleansed* (Luke 17:11-14).

7. In Jesus' day, a person with leprosy would have been treated as
    an outcast—it was contagious, and people lived in fear of
    catching it. A person with HIV/AIDS today may also receive
    this response from people. What do the verses you have stud-
    ied so far tell you about how Jesus would respond to a person
    with HIV/AIDS?

    _____

    _____

    _____

8. HIV and AIDS can be a result of sinful behavior. However, like
    Jesus, we need to live according to God's standard of truth
    while having compassion for those who might be suffering as
    a result of their actions. Christ wasn't afraid to reach out to
    people whom others classified as untouchable or forgotten.
    As we saw in Mark 2:15-17, He sought out those who needed
    Him—those who knew they were sinners and needed His heal-
    ing touch. What do you think this story about Jesus at Levi's
    house would look like today if He were spending time with
    HIV/AIDS victims? What would people who lack His compas-
    sion say about His actions?

    _____

    _____

    _____

9. Beyond their physical suffering, in what ways was Jesus interested in the people who were sick?

_____

_____

_____

_____

apply

Now it is time to take both truth and compassion and put them into action. If you are a follower of Jesus, you have a great opportunity to be truth and compassion to those who are hurting. You have a great opportunity to let those suffering from diseases such as HIV/AIDS know that Jesus cares about what they are facing.

1. Review what you have learned about HIV/AIDS. How has this information helped you understand this disease?

_____

_____

_____

2. Look at the risk factors for contracting HIV. In what ways are teens the most at risk?

_____

_____

_____

3. How can words of truth spoken in love save lives?

_____

_____

_____

4. What misconceptions about HIV/AIDS do you think keep people from showing love and compassion to its victims?

5. Knowing how Jesus felt about the sick and the "sinners," how will your view of those who are hurting change?

6. There may be students in your youth group who are affected by HIV and AIDS. Why is it important for them to receive love and compassion from your group? What was Jesus goal in showing love and compassion?

7. As previously stated, sometimes HIV/AIDS come about as a result of sin. How can your group take a stand for what is right, yet point suffering group members to God's forgiveness and love? (Note: All sinful behavior is wrong—a person who has contracted HIV through a sinful act is not less valuable than a person who has told a lie, stolen something or been disrespectful to his or her parents.)

reflect

Are you at risk? It is important to look at yourself and see if you are making choices that put you in danger of contracting HIV (or a host of other STDs). This is the truth part. It can be difficult to face up to these facts, but it could save your life, protect your future (and your future spouse and children), and deepen your relationship with God.

1. After reading the information in the starter section, is it possible you have been exposed to HIV?

   _____
   _____
   _____

2. If you have been or are sexually active, have you ever been tested for HIV and other STDs?

   _____
   _____
   _____

Please remember that if you do test positive for HIV, it may have just saved your life—but only if you take the test results seriously and get the help you need. If you have been sexually active, you should be tested (sometimes repeatedly over several months). Yet being sexually active has emotional and spiritual consequences as well. Consider the story of Tonisha:

> I lost my virginity at 19. Since I waited longer than most of my friends, and they all seemed "fine," I didn't think it was a big deal to have sex. During my freshman year of

college, I met the man I thought I would marry. We talked about where we would marry and who would be there and the type of ring I wanted. With all this conversation, I figured he was for sure "the one" and having sex was somehow more justified. Two years later we still weren't married and I still didn't have a ring. What I did have was my OB/GYN office calling me. . . . I have HPV [human papillomavirus] . . . . The boy is no longer in the picture and life feels dismal. Ironically, it isn't only because I have to tell my future spouse, but because every day I remember that special part of myself that I sacrificed. . . . Even if I hadn't gotten HPV, I'd still have to deal with all of the other consequences, including those to my heart and my soul, because I didn't honor God's boundary for sex.[4]

3. How can being sexually active outside of marriage cause you emotional suffering?

_____

_____

_____

4. To whom can you talk if you have doubts or questions?

_____

_____

_____

Note that if you have a serious problem, your parents need to know. Laying out the truth might be difficult, but it will free you to effectively deal with any problems you may be having. Even if they get mad, they will be your strongest support. Your youth pastor or another trusted adult is also another place you can turn.

5. What have you learned about Jesus that could help you deal with a situation like this?

_____

_____

_____

6. What choices can you make today to protect yourself and to have compassion toward those who have or are at risk of contracting HIV or other STDs?

_____

_____

_____

7. If you have a friend who is a victim of HIV/AIDS, what can you do to show them Jesus' love and compassion?

_____

_____

_____

meditation

Then they cried to the LORD in their trouble, and he saved them from their distress. He sent out his word and healed them; he rescued them from the grave.

PSALM 107:19-20

Notes
1. Information is paraphrased from an article by Mary-Ann Shafer, M.D., and Florence Isaacs, "Teenagers and AIDS," *Good Housekeeping*, May 1990.
2 "Basic Information about HIV and AIDS," Centers for Disease Control and Prevention (CDC), April 2012. www.cdc.gov/hiv/topics/basic/.
3. Pam Stenzel and Melissa Nesdahl, *Nobody Told Me* (Ventura, CA: Regal, 2010), p. 71.
4. Ibid., p. 80.

the crisis of pornography

Each of you should learn to control your own body in a way that is holy and honorable, not in passionate lust like the pagans, who do not know God; and that in this matter no one should wrong or take advantage of a brother or sister. The Lord will punish all those who commit such sins, as we told you and warned you. For God did not call us to be impure, but to live a holy life.

1 THESSALONIANS 4:4-7

Kevin had been active in his church's middle school ministry for more than three years. He was an excellent musician, and the students loved how he jammed on the guitar. Kevin was a friendly, easygoing leader who spent hour after hour with young teens. He was popular and eager to help out, and the kids looked up to him. What he appeared to be on the outside, however, deceptively hid his secret life on the inside.

The shock came when police investigators arrived at Kevin's church to ask the junior and senior high pastors about his suspicious behavior. To their horror, disbelief and sadness, Kevin was being indicted for trafficking pornographic material. He was a link in a major pornography ring. His secret life had been publicly exposed.

Pornography destroys the lives of every person exposed to its addictive tentacles. It degrades and cheapens those made in God's image. It violates those who make it, those who watch it, and the innocent victims who suffer its destructive effects. Pornography kills the human spirit because it seeks to possess and manipulate what God has made holy. Pornography kills the joy-filled life God intended for every person. It is a wildfire of destruction.

You can help young people deal with their sexuality in a positive way by helping them understand the dangers of pornography. Pornography is rarely talked about in the Church, but there are thousands of young people who struggle with what they see on TV, movies, video games and the Internet. You can help young people by exposing pornography for what it is and teaching what the Bible tells us about our sexuality.

Though debased, pornography is a theological statement. It says: There is
no God who says I should limit my lust or channel my passion or give
as well as get. . . . Pornography is anti-woman and anti-child. It is anti-marriage
and anti-permanence. Thus it is profoundly anti-civilization. Since civilization
is a social support to the dynamics of life, pornography is anti-life.

WILLIAM STANMEYER

the crisis of
pornography

starter

PORNOGRAPHY QUESTIONS: Copy and distribute the following quiz to your group members to see what they know about pornography and its effects on teens.

T F

__ __ 1. The compulsive use of porn dulls the ability of the brain to experience pleasure.

__ __ 2. Exposure to porn in children distorts their mental, emotional and social development.

__ __ 3. Soft porn (still pictures of nude/partially nude individuals or couples or portrayals of sex in R-rated movies) is not addictive, and occasional use is not a problem.

Note: You can download this group study guide in 8½" x 11" format at **www.gospellight.com/uncommon/dealing_with_stress_and_crisis.zip.**

T　F

___ ___ 4. Pornography is a safe alternative for dealing with over-whelming feelings that come with hormone changes during puberty.

___ ___ 5. Pornography is a beautiful display of God's creation.

___ ___ 6. God is anti-sex.

___ ___ 7. Viewing pornography causes an endorphin release that is 5 to 7 times more addictive than cocaine.

___ ___ 8. Pornography is only a problem for boys and men.

___ ___ 9. Technology has made pornography accessible to everyone.

___ ___10. Soft porn use often leads to hard-core porn use.

___ ___11. Pornography producers target children and teens using website search terms they are likely to enter.

___ ___12. Sexting is not pornography.

___ ___13. A person who sends or receives sexting messages involving a minor is breaking laws and can be arrested and charged with a crime.

___ ___14. The most important sex organ is your mind.

___ ___15. Pornography dehumanizes and devalues people and makes it more difficult for those who are exposed to it to build healthy relationships.

___ ___16. Ten percent of search engine requests are pornography related.

Once everyone has completed the quiz, take a few moments to go over the answers as a group.[1]

1. **True.** This leads to an addictive need for increasingly greater amounts of stimulation to give the same sense of sexual satisfaction.[2]

2. **True.** Exposure to porn in children distorts each of these things.[3]

3. **False.** Soft porn use is addictive.[4]

4. **False.** Using pornography is like a chemical bath for the brain, and it creates more of a struggle for those using it than just managing changing hormones.

5. **False.** Pornography violates God's purpose in making our physical bodies attractive to the opposite sex. Pornography eliminates God's boundary of marriage and the elements of an emotional and spiritual relationship with the other person.

6. **False.** God created sex. He is PRO-SEX and intends it to be an experience that draws a husband and wife closer to Him and binds them to each other. Anything less cheapens it and isn't part of what He wants for people.

7. **True.** How does this change your perspective of its harmfulness?

8. **False.** The number of girls and women struggling with pornography is growing rapidly.

9. **True.** The ease of access to pornography brought about by technology has made protecting yourself more difficult and unhealthy secrecy easier to maintain.

10. **True.** Every addiction starts with what seems like a harmless, one-time action.

11. **True.** Pornography producers target children and teens in this way.

12. **False.** Pornography is defined as "the depiction of erotic behavior (as in pictures or writing) intended to cause sexual excitement."[5] Consider the purpose of sexting.

13. **True.** In 2009, six Pennsylvania high school students were faced with child pornography charges after three teenage girls allegedly took nude or seminude pictures of themselves and shared them with male classmates.[6]

14. **True.** Once an image enters the brain, it is there forever. Pornography can affect how your brain—the center of your physical and emotional functions—works, and it can damage your ability to bond with one partner.

15. **True.** Pornography separates sex from its primary purpose and reduces it to self-indulgent recreation. More than this, there is a whole world of people caught in the production of pornography who are victimized.

16. **False.** Right now, the number is closer to 25 percent.

Ask the group to briefly discuss any of the facts they found the most surprising or that impacted their perception of the damage pornography can wield.

message

You have just been given a crash course in the impact that pornography can have on a person. It is also important to recognize that pornography takes something God created as good and twists it into something evil.

God's intentions for sex

The Bible speaks strongly about sexual immorality as sin. It also identifies God's intention for sex as something to be enjoyed within the context of marriage as an expression of the deep loving bond shared by a husband and wife. We see this intent in Genesis 1:26-27,31:

> Then God said, "Let us make man in our image, in our likeness, and let them rule over the fish of the sea and the birds of the air, over the livestock, over all the earth, and over all the creatures that move

along the ground." So God created man in his own image, in the im-
age of God he created him; male and female he created them. . . .
God saw all that he had made, and it was very good.

1. What did God use as a model for His creation of humans?

2. What do these verses tell you about how God felt about His creation?

the bondage of pornography

Pornography is addictive. It puts people in bondage to sin and pulls them away from God. In Galatians 5:1, Paul describes this bondage:

It is for freedom that Christ has set us free. Stand firm, then, and do not let yourselves be burdened again by a yoke of slavery.

1. According to this verse, why did Christ set us free?

2. How are we told to respond to things that try to enslave us?

In Ephesians 4:17-24, Paul provides a great description of the differences between a person who is enslaved to sin and one who has found freedom in Christ:

> *So I tell you this, and insist on it in the Lord, that you must no longer live as the Gentiles do, in the futility of their thinking. They are darkened in their understanding and separated from the life of God because of the ignorance that is in them due to the hardening of their hearts. Having lost all sensitivity, they have given themselves over to sensuality so as to indulge in every kind of impurity, with a continual lust for more. You, however, did not come to know Christ that way. Surely you heard of him and were taught in him in accordance with the truth that is in Jesus. You were taught, with regard to your former way of life, to put off your old self, which is being corrupted by its deceitful desires; to be made new in the attitude of your minds; and to put on the new self, created to be like God in true righteousness and holiness.*

3. How does addictive behavior affect a person?

4. What instructions does Paul give to the person who wants to be free from his or her addiction?

5. Where is the first place this person needs to be made new?

_____

_____

_____

freedom from addiction

To find freedom from the addiction or burden of sin, we need help. In Matthew 11:28-30, Jesus tells us how to get the help we need to let go of burdens in our lives such as pornography:

> *Come to me, all you who are weary and burdened, and I will give you rest. Take my yoke upon you and learn from me, for I am gentle and humble in heart, and you will find rest for your souls. For my yoke is easy and my burden is light.*

1. What does Jesus ask you to do?

_____

_____

_____

2. What does He offer you in return?

_____

_____

_____

3. A "yoke" is a wooden beam shaped to fit two animals so they can pull a heavy load together. What is the difference between the "yoke" of bondage to sin and the "yoke" that Jesus offers?

_____

_____

_____

the human cost of pornography

Pornography exploits and dehumanizes people for the sake of lust. God has a tender heart for the vulnerable. In a parable Jesus told in Matthew 25:40, He says, "Whatever you did for one of the least of these brothers of mine, you did for me."

1. What does our treatment of those who are vulnerable say about our relationship with God?

   _____

   _____

   _____

2. Who is the exploitation of "the least of these" an attack on?

   _____

   _____

   _____

Sexual immorality has a huge impact on human relationships. In Colossians 3:5,12,14, Paul writes:

> *Put to death, therefore, whatever belongs to your earthly nature: sexual immorality, impurity, lust, evil desires and greed . . . clothe yourselves with compassion, kindness, humility, gentleness and patience. . . . And over all these virtues put on love, which binds them all together in perfect unity.*

3. What does Paul say we put to death? What does he say we should "clothe ourselves" with or adopt?

   _____

   _____

   _____

4. What is the impact of putting on love in our relationships with others?

5. What is the impact of the opposite—of allowing sexual immorality, impurity, lust, evil desires and greed to affect our relationships with others?

dig

1. God wants His best for us—which is only available through a relationship with Him as He describes for us in His Word, the Bible. How is pornography an attack on the image of God created in us?

2. How does this attack affect the value we place on the people God has created?

3. Addiction enslaves us, but Christ sets us free. What does it mean to have "freedom in Christ"?

    _____

    _____

    _____

4. How does sharing Jesus' "yoke" allow us to be free (see Matthew 11:28-30)?

    _____

    _____

    _____

5. How does the yoke of slavery impact us? What is our source of freedom (see Galatians 5:1)?

    _____

    _____

    _____

    _____

6. Review Ephesians 4:17-24. How does belonging to Jesus help us win the battle we are fighting in our minds against pornography and sexual immorality?

    _____

    _____

    _____

7. How does addictive behavior affect a person's relationship with God?

    _____

    _____

    _____

8. What does it mean to care for "the least of these" (see Matthew 25:40)?

_____

_____

_____

_____

9. Why is it important for us to build healthy human relationships—for ourselves and for the world in which we live?

_____

_____

_____

_____

apply

1. The issue of pornography has global impact. Take a few minutes to look at your slice of the world and evaluate how pornography has impacted your community, school, friends and family. What are the primary ways teens are exposed to pornography?

_____

_____

_____

_____

2. Why do you think some teens have difficulty seeing the dangers of pornography?

_____

_____

_____

_____

3. Why do most teens think they can avoid becoming addicted, yet indulge in using pornography?

4. What do you think of the fact that pornographic images, once seen, are permanently part of a person's memory?

5. In what ways do you see the world's view of sex and the value of women influencing teenagers' attitudes toward each other?

6. How would having God's view of sex affect the quality of your relationships with the opposite sex? With your future spouse?

7. Herbert Case, a former Detroit police inspector, once said, "There has not been a sex murder in the history of our department in which a killer was not an avid reader of lewd magazines."[7] Do you agree with his statement? Why or why not?

8. What are the benefits of guarding your eyes and mind against pornography and the attitudes it promotes?

9. What hope do you see for those who need to break the influence of pornography in their lives? What help does God offer?

10. How can teens impact their communities in fighting pornography? How can your efforts point others toward God and His love for people?

reflect

1. Do you believe pornography can be addictive? Why or why not?

2. Have you ever been exposed to pornography? If so, how did this affect your heart and mind?

3. What are some rules you can set for yourself that will help you to keep each area listed below "pornography-free"?

Music: _____

_____

_____

_____

TV: _____

_____

_____

_____

Movies: _____

_____

_____

_____

Video games: _____

_____

_____

_____

The Internet: _____

_____

_____

_____

Books and magazines: _____

_____

_____

Relationships with friends: _____

_____

_____

_____

4. Who can you talk to if you have questions or are struggling in this area? (Note that secrecy is a barrier to overcoming a problem like this, so consider talking to a trusted adult about finding help and support.)

_____

_____

_____

_____

5. Take a few minutes to talk to God about any struggle you are having with pornography. Confess it all to Him and ask for forgiveness. Ask Him to help you in these areas, and then seek out the support of a trusted adult. How can you likewise help a friend who is struggling with pornography?

_____

_____

_____

_____

6. If a friend told you that he or she was into pornography, what would you say to that person about what God wants for him or her?

_____

_____

_____

_____

7. How can you raise awareness among your friends about the damage that pornography can do to them personally?

meditation

Since you are my rock and my fortress, for the sake of your name lead and guide me. Keep me free from the trap that is set for me, for you are my refuge. Into your hands I commit my spirit; deliver me, LORD, my faithful God.

PSALM 31:3-5

Notes

1. Unless otherwise noted, the information in this section is adapted from *A Guide to What One Person Can Do About Pornography* by the American Family Association. www.afa.net/uploaded Files/FAQ/PornGuide.pdf.
2. Matt Fradd, "The Teen Porn Epidemic . . . and What to Do About It," The Catholic Exchange, June 7, 2012. http://catholicexchange.com/the-teen-porn-epidemic-and-what-to-do-about-it/
3. Ibid.
4. Pam Stenzel and Melissa Nesdahl, *Who's In Your Social Network?* (Ventura, CA: Regal, 2011), pp. 83-98.
5. Merriam-Webster, s.v. "pornography." http://www.merriam-webster.com/dictionary/pornography.
6. Mike Brunker, "Sexting Surprise: Teens Face Child Porn Charges," NBC News, January 15, 2009. http://www.msnbc.msn.com/id/28679588/ns/technology_and_science-tech_and_gadgets/t/sexting-surprise-teens-face-child-porn-charges/#.UO3bnbbeT8A.
7. Herbert Case, quoted in *A Guide to What One Person Can Do About Pornography*, p. 10.

unit III
helping friends in crisis

Perhaps the greatest "discovery" in the history of recent youth ministry is the incredible effectiveness of peer ministry and peer counseling. Previously, these terms were more widely accepted within the secular community than among Christian educators. However, today we know that often the most effective ministry is accomplished on a peer-to-peer or friend-to-friend level.

At a winter camp I attended some time ago, they had scheduled one of the finest youth speakers in the world to talk to the high school students. He did a great job presenting the gospel of Jesus Christ to the kids. The youth staff kept saying, "This is some of the finest speaking we've ever heard."

On Sunday morning, before the main session began, the kids in the camp taught some seminars themselves. One girl named Lisa taught a session on self-image. It wasn't a polished presentation. Lisa had a ton of Scriptures and shared her personal struggles, but the body and content of her material was really weak.

At the end of the retreat, the students wrote evaluations of their experiences. It was almost shocking to see that even though the kids did like the big-time speaker, they liked Lisa's seminar even more. Why? Student after student remarked that they could really relate to what Lisa was going through in her own life and faith journey. Peer ministry wins again!

One of your most important jobs as a youth worker is to cultivate peer ministry. If you can teach your students how to minister and counsel their friends, you will have gone a long way toward developing a lifestyle of servanthood in their lives. Our job is to create doers of the Word and not just hearers, and this section is intended to inspire your kids to be people helpers in the same manner as Jesus helped His friends minister to the people of Palestine.

Consider the old Chinese proverb, "Give a man a fish and feed him for a day; teach a man to fish and feed him for a lifetime." In a sense, that's what this unit is all about. You have the opportunity to give your students some lifelong skills and to inspire them to be more effective people helpers with the skills of counseling, problem solving, active listening and a better understanding of two of life's most critical issues: death and dying.

These sessions have been tested with junior-high and senior-high students and, hopefully, will be a lot of fun. However, anytime you bring up crisis situations, you have to be prepared for horror stories as well. Statistics tell us that no matter your group's size, denomination or theological perspective, these crisis issues have affected or will affect your students.

Thank you for tackling the not-so-easy task of helping kids deal with the more difficult issues of life. You are making a difference and are to be commended for your courage. God bless you.

how to be there for a friend

Two are better than one, because they have a good return for their work:
If one falls down, his friend can help him up. But pity the man who falls and has
no one to help him up! Also, if two lie down together, they will keep warm.
But how can one keep warm alone? Though one may be overpowered, two can
defend themselves. A cord of three strands is not quickly broken.

ECCLESIASTES 4:9-12

"Michael, what's going on? Why are you giving me all your favorite CDs, your iPod and baseball card collection? You love this stuff! Why are you giving it to me?"

"No reason, Anthony. I just want you to have it."

"*Michael* . . ."

"Okay, I'll tell you why, but you have to promise not to tell anyone. I mean, if you're really my friend, you've got to swear you won't tell anyone what I'm going to tell you."

"Sure, Michael. You know I can keep a promise. We're buds, right? But why all the secrecy about you giving me your stuff?"

Anthony doesn't realize what he's just promised Michael. He doesn't understand what Michael's about to do. Anthony has never known anyone—let alone his best friend—who was on the verge of committing suicide. Anthony doesn't have a clue how to help him.

Friends helping friends. That's an important and vital role you have as a youth worker. You are a coach, instructor, trainer and guide in teaching young people how to help their friends. In crisis situations, your influence can play a critical yet invisible role in saving the life of a teenager.

Take Anthony, for example. If Anthony attended your youth ministry and happened to hear a talk on how to help a suicidal friend, he would be equipped to save Michael's life instead of being an accomplice to end it. Anthony would know the clues and signals a suicidal friend gives out before that person ends his or her life. He would be suspicious about Michael's ongoing depression and why his is suddenly giving away his favorite things. Anthony would know how to save his best friend's life.

Teaching the students in your youth ministry how to help their friends can literally mean the difference between life and death. The Bible is filled with practical skills students can easily incorporate into their faith and friendships. Never underestimate the power of God in your life and the significant influence you have in helping your students help their friends.

God has called each of us to receive His life and to give His life away. When you help students help their friends, you do just that.

Sorrow is like a precious treasure shown only to friends.
AFRICAN PROVERB

how to be there for a friend

starter

CRAZY QUIZ: It's time for a bit lighter starter activity, so make copies of the following crazy quiz and hand it out to your group members.[1]

1. If you went to bed at 8 AM and set the alarm to get up at 9 AM the next morning, how many hours of sleep would you get?
2. Does England have a Fourth of July?
3. Why can't a man living in Winston-Salem, North Carolina, be buried west of the Mississippi River?
4. If you had a match and entered a room in which there was a kerosene lamp, an oil heater, and a wood burning stove, which would you light first?

Note: You can download this group study guide in 8½" x 11" format at **www.gospellight.com/uncommon/dealing_with_stress_and_crisis.zip.**

5. Some months have 30 days, some have 31 days, how many months have 28 days?

6. A man builds a house with four sides to it, and it is rectangular in shape. Each side has a southern exposure. A big bear comes wandering by. What color is the bear?

7. How far can a dog run into the woods?

8. What four words appear on every denomination of U.S. coin?

9. What is the minimum number of baseball players on the field during any part of an inning in a regular game?

10. You have in your hand two U.S. coins that total 55 cents in value. One is not a nickel. What are the two coins?

11. A farmer had 17 sheep, and all but 9 died. How many does he have left?

12. Divide 30 by one-half and add 10. What is the answer?

13. Take two apples from three apples. What do you have?

14. An archeologist claimed he found some gold coins dated "46 BC" Do you think he really did? Explain.

15. A woman gives a beggar 50 cents. The woman is the beggar's sister, but the beggar is not the woman's brother. How come?

16. How many animals of each species did Moses take aboard the Ark with him?

17. Is it illegal in North Carolina for a man to marry his widow's sister? Why?

18. What word in this test is mispelled?

19. From what animal do we get whale bones?

20. Where was Paul going on the road to Damascus?

When everyone is finished, go over the answers:

1. One hour; the alarm would ring on the first occurrence of 9 AM

2. Yes; July has 31 days for everyone

3. Because he's not dead yet
4. The match
5. 12; they all do
6. White; for all for sides of the house to have a southern exposure, you would have to be sitting on the North Pole
7. Halfway; for the other half he's running out
8. "United States of America" or "In God We Trust"
9. Ten players—nine outfielders and a batter
10. A 50-cent piece and a nickel—one is not a nickel, but the other is
11. Nine
12. Seventy; $30 \div .5 = 60$, $+10 = 70$
13. Two
14. No; a coin could not be dated "bc" because it was before Christ was born
15. They are sisters
16. None; Noah took the animals, not Moses
17. Because he is dead
18. "Misspelled"
19. Whale
20. Damascus

Award a prize for the person with the most correct answers. Briefly discuss what skills were helpful in answering these questions (such as careful listening, math, Bible knowledge, spelling, history, and common sense).

message

The Bible is packed with great advice on how to be there for your friends and help them in a crisis. Knowing what the Bible says about helping others will prepare you to respond if you are ever in a situation where you need to help a friend through a difficult circumstance. Read each section of Scripture below and identify the advice it gives that can help you be ready when a friend is in need.

> *Trust in the* LORD *with all your heart and lean not on your own understanding; in all your ways acknowledge him, and he will make your paths straight* (Proverbs 3:5-6).

1. What do these verses say to do? What do they say to *not* do?

    _____

    _____

    _____

2. How does this relate to being there for friends? What is the first thing you should you do when you see a friend in trouble?

    _____

    _____

    _____

> *Not only so, but we also rejoice in our sufferings, because we know that suffering produces perseverance; perseverance, character; and character, hope. And hope does not disappoint us, because God has poured out his love into our hearts by the Holy Spirit, whom he has given us* (Romans 5:3-5).

3. What attitude toward suffering does Paul describe?

    _____

    _____

    _____

4. How can the suffering you experienced and the perseverance you needed to get through that situation be a tool to help someone in crisis?

_____

_____

_____

_____

And we urge you, brothers, warn those who are idle, encourage the timid, help the weak, be patient with everyone (1 Thessalonians 5:14).

5. What three commands does Paul give in this verse? Who does he direct to take these actions?

_____

_____

_____

6. What do these words say about being there for a friend in crisis?

_____

_____

_____

Everyone should be quick to listen, slow to speak and slow to become angry, for man's anger does not bring about the righteous life that God desires (James 1:19).

7. What skills does James describe in these verses?

_____

_____

_____

8. How will using these skills enable you to better help your friends? (Note: "righteous" in the Bible can be thought of as one whose life is aligned with what God wants—one who, by faith, seeks to do God's will.)

_____

_____

_____

dig

There are different ways to use knowledge. When a friend is in crisis, you need wisdom to know what information to share, when to be quiet and listen and when to ask for help from others. Turning to God first will give you the wisdom to make choices that will help you touch the life of your friend in a healthy way.

look for signs of trouble

One of the most important skills needed in helping your friends is an ability to see that a problem exists. Sometimes, people are so overwhelmed that they might not even realize that they are in a crisis. Consider the case of Moses in the Bible. Moses was an amazing leader who had been given the important task of leading the Israelites out of Egypt and into the Promised Land. Yet even he needed help from a friend to see that was pushing himself too hard. As we read in Exodus 18:13-23:

> *The next day Moses took his seat to serve as judge for the people, and they stood around him from morning till evening. When his father-in-law saw all that Moses was doing for the people, he said, "What is this you are doing for the people? Why do you alone sit as judge, while all these people stand around you from morning till evening?"*

Moses answered him, "Because the people come to me to seek God's will. Whenever they have a dispute, it is brought to me, and I decide between the parties and inform them of God's decrees and laws."

Moses' father-in-law replied, "What you are doing is not good. You and these people who come to you will only wear yourselves out. The work is too heavy for you; you cannot handle it alone. Listen now to me and I will give you some advice, and may God be with you. You must be the people's representative before God and bring their disputes to him. Teach them the decrees and laws, and show them the way to live and the duties they are to perform. But select capable men from all the people—men who fear God, trustworthy men who hate dishonest gain—and appoint them as officials over thousands, hundreds, fifties and tens. Have them serve as judges for the people at all times, but have them bring every difficult case to you; the simple cases they can decide themselves. That will make your load lighter, because they will share it with you. If you do this and God so commands, you will be able to stand the strain, and all these people will go home satisfied."

1. What problem was Jethro able to identify?

2. What reasons did Jethro give for why what Moses was doing was "not good"?

3. What advice did Jethro give to Moses? How would this advice help Moses be more effective in helping the people?

    _____

    _____

    _____

4. What would taking this advice require Moses to do on his part?

    _____

    _____

    _____

seek wisdom from God

Once you see that there is a problem, you need to ask God for wisdom and guidance in how you can best help.

> *The fear of the LORD is the beginning of wisdom; all who follow his precepts have good understanding. To him belongs eternal praise* (Psalm 111:10).

> *For the LORD gives wisdom, and from his mouth come knowledge and understanding* (Proverbs 2:6).

1. What do these verses tell you about the source of true wisdom?

    _____

    _____

    _____

2. What does God promise to those who seek Him for wisdom?

    _____

    _____

    _____

3. Why do you need wisdom from God when a friend is in crisis?

_____

_____

_____

_____

next steps in being there for a friend

Once you have recognized a problem and sought wisdom from the Lord on how best to help, you are ready to step into the situation. Here are 10 principles to keep in mind as you take this next crucial step:

1. Believe that God can use you to help others, just as He has helped you. Rely upon Him.
2. Understand that silence is okay.
3. If you feel you must speak, ask questions.
4. A major indicator of your maturity is your ability to listen.
5. Remain calm and caring.
6. Don't have a judgmental spirit.
7. Remember that confidentiality is vital.
8. Be prepared to seek additional help and support in referring the person to a professional.
9. Provide an optimistic relationship.
10. If you are helping a person solve a problem, remember that he or she must own the solution. Don't enable the person.[1]

1. What skills will help you apply these principles?

_____

_____

_____

_____

2. How are your attitudes and actions connected when you are helping a friend?

_____

_____

_____

_____

3. How is knowing God's Word part of being prepared to help a friend in crisis? How will the Holy Spirit help you (see Mark 13:10-12)?

_____

_____

_____

_____

4. Sometimes, your friends will be in crisis because of certain behaviors they have chosen to do, and "enabling" them (helping in a way that makes it easier for them to continue doing those behaviors) will be destructive. Why is it critical that the person "owns" the solution?

_____

_____

_____

_____

5. How can you safeguard against enabling your friends?

_____

_____

_____

_____

6. How is knowing God's Word part of being prepared to help a friend? How will the Holy Spirit help you (see Mark 13:10-12)?

---

apply

1. Each person is unique in his or her strengths and weaknesses, but the skills to help a friend in crisis can always be improved with time, effort, support from others, insight from God's Word and prayer. What helping skills come most easily for you?

---

2. Which helping skills do you need to work on most?

---

3. What can friends do to help each other work on these skills?

---

4. What can you do to be better equipped through prayer and God's Word?

    ----

5. When helping friends, it is important to have them talk about their feelings and get in touch with how they are feeling. Some people express feelings easily, while others have real difficulty in sharing. The Intensity of Feelings Chart on the following pages can be a helpful tool to use in helping people identify their feelings and the intensity of their emotions. Read the chart and then write words from it that describe what someone might be feeling in each of the following situations.

    My dad and mom are getting a divorce.

    I was sexually abused when I was 11 years old.

    My best friend attempted suicide last night.

    ----

intensity of feelings chart

strong

Happy	Caring	Depressed	Inadequate	Fearful
thrilled	tenderness	desolate	worthless	terrified
on cloud nine	toward	dejected	good for nothing	frightened
	affection for	hopeless		intimidated
ecstatic	captivated by	alienated	powerless	horrified
overjoyed	attached to	depressed	helpless	desperate
excited	devoted to	gloomy	impotent	panicky
elated	adoration	dismal	crippled	terror
sensational	loving	bleak	inferior	stricken
exhilarated	infatuated	in despair	emasculated	stage fright
fantastic	enamored	empty	useless	dread
terrific	cherished	barren	finished	vulnerable
top of the world	idolize	grieved	like a failure	paralyzed
	worship	grief	washed-up	
turned on		despair		
euphoric		grim		
enthusiastic				
delighted				
marvelous				
great				

Confused	Hurt	Angry	Lonely	Guilt/Shame
bewildered	crushed	furious	isolated	sick at heart
puzzled	destroyed	enraged	abandoned	unforgivable
baffled	ruined	seething	all alone	humiliated
perplexed	degraded	outraged	forsaken	disgraced
trapped	pain(ed)	infuriated	cut off	degraded

Confused	Hurt	Angry	Lonely	Guilt/Shame
confounded	wounded	burned up		horrible
in a dilemma	devastated	hateful		mortified
befuddled	tortured	fighting mad		exposed
in a quandary	disgraced	nauseated		
full of questions	humiliated	violent		
	anguished	indignant		
confused	at mercy of	hatred		
	cast off	galled		
	forsaken	vengeful		
	rejected			
	discarded			

moderate

Happy	Caring	Depressed	Inadequate	Fearful
cheerful	caring	distressed	inadequate	afraid
lighthearted	fond of	upset	whipped	scared
happy	regard	downcast	defeated	fearful
serene	respectful	sorrowful	incompetent	apprehensive
wonderful	admiration	demoralized	inept	jumpy
up	concern for	discouraged	overwhelmed	shaky
aglow	hold dear	miserable	ineffective	threatened
glowing	prize	pessimistic	lacking	distrustful
in high spirits	taken with	tearful	deficient	risky
	turned on	weepy	unable	alarmed
jovial	trust	rotten	incapable	butterflies
riding high	close	awful	small	awkward
elevated		horrible	insignificant	defensive
neat		terrible	no good	

Happy	Caring	Depressed	Inadequate	Fearful
		blue	immobilized	
		lost	unfit	
		melancholy	unimportant	
			incomplete	

Confused	Hurt	Angry	Lonely	Guilt/Shame
mixed-up	hurt	resentful	lonely	ashamed
disorganized	belittled	irritated	alienated	guilty
foggy	shot down	hostile	estranged	remorseful
troubled	overlooked	annoyed	remote	crummy
adrift	abused	upset with	alone	to blame
lost	depreciated	agitated	apart from others	lost face
at loose ends	criticized	mad		demeaned
	defamed	aggravated	insulated from others	
going in circles	censured	offended		
	discredited	antagonistic		
disconcerted	disparaged	exasperated		
frustrated	laughed at	belligerent		
flustered	maligned	mean		
in a bind	mistreated	vexed		
ambivalent	ridiculed	spiteful		
disturbed	devalued	vindictive		
helpless	scorned			
embroiled	mocked			
	scoffed at			
	used			
	exploited			
	debased			

Confused	Hurt	Angry	Lonely	Guilt/Shame
	slammed			
	slandered			
	impugned			
	cheapened			

mild

Happy	Caring	Depressed	Inadequate	Fearful
glad	warm toward	unhappy	lacking confidence	nervous
good		down		anxious
contented	friendly	low	unsure of yourself	unsure
satisfied	like	bad		hesitant
gratified	positive toward	blah	uncertain	timid
pleasant		disappointed	weak	shy
pleased		sad	inefficient	worried
fine		glum		uneasy
				bashful

Confused	Hurt	Angry	Lonely	Guilt/Shame
uncertain	put down	uptight	left out	regretful
unsure	neglected	disgusted	excluded	wrong
bothered	overlooked	bugged	lonesome	embarrassed
uncom-fortable	minimized	turned off	distant	at fault
	let down	put out	aloof	in error
undecided	not appreciated	miffed		responsible for
		irked		
	taken for granted	ticked off		blew it
		perturbed		

I had the best birthday ever.

I studied like crazy and my teacher only gave me a C on the exam.

I honestly could kill myself right now.

We went "all the way."

I drank a little too much at the party.

I feel far away from God.

I've been thinking about running away.

_____

_____

_____

_____

I'm embarrassed because of my weight.

_____

_____

_____

_____

I can't stop looking at pornography.

_____

_____

_____

_____

reflect

1. A crisis is usually a matter of perception. Some people "stress out" over getting pimples, while others don't worry much even during traumatic experiences. How would you describe how you handle stress?

_____

_____

_____

_____

2. What types of things keep you from helping a friend in crisis?

    ....
    ....
    ....
    ....

3. What type of training do you wish you had to handle crises
   better?

    ....
    ....
    ....
    ....

4. James states, "But be doers of the word, and not hearers only"
   (James 1:22, *NKJV*). When a friend is in need, you have the
   chance to be there for him or her. Fill in the blanks below
   about one person or family whom you know is in a crisis.

   Who:

    ....
    ....
    ....

   Now you need to develop a plan to help. Answer the following
   questions, and decide if you need input from an adult to accomplish your plan.

   What will I do:

    ....
    ....
    ....

When will I do it:

_____
_____
_____

Where will I do it:

_____
_____
_____

How will I do it:

_____
_____
_____

Next, pray about it. Take the problem and your plan to God. When you are ready, go do it!

meditation

I can do everything through him who gives me strength.

PHILIPPIANS 4:13

Notes

1. Mike Yokanelli and Wayne Rice, *Ideas Numbers 13-16* (El Cajon, CA: Youth Specialties, 1981), p. 11.
2. These principles are taken from the National Institute of Youth Ministry's Peer Leadership Training for student leaders developed by Chris Cannon.

how to counsel a friend

Your statutes are my delight; they are my counselors.
PSALM 119:24

Stephanie and Danae were getting ready to drive home after spending three hours in a local coffee shop catching up on one another's lives. "Danae," Stephanie said as she got up, "there's one more thing I need to tell you. It's been tearing me up all night, and you're the only one I can trust with this."

"Go ahead, Stephanie," said Danae. "You can tell me anything."

"Remember the guy, John, I told you about tonight? Well, after a couple months of dating we began sleeping together, and just last week I found out I was pregnant. I couldn't believe it. I was so scared. My parents would have killed me if they found out. So, last Friday, I went to the clinic and had an abortion."

Stephanie broke down in tears and crumpled into Danae's arms. She went on to explain her intense feelings of guilt, confusion, sorrow and anger over the whole situation. Danae's care and compassion made Stephanie feel safe in the midst of her pain. This wasn't the first time a friend had trusted Danae with such sensitive information. Everyone knew they could trust her.

Does your youth ministry have a "Danae"? Although she isn't a trained professional counselor, her peers respect her and know she listens and understands. She is widely regarded for her Christlike compassion and empathy for those in pain. Danae is a peer counselor who has brought healing to many of her friends' lives.

One of the unfortunate myths of counseling is that only professionals are equipped to help others. In fact, teenagers can be extremely helpful and gifted counselors. Watch the "Danaes" in your life and witness this myth being debunked.

Encouraging your students to be counselors and ministers to their friends is an incredible way to unleash the power of Christ on their campuses. When you teach biblical ministry skills to students, you equip them for a lifetime of significant Kingdom work. One of the most critical measuring sticks of a healthy youth ministry is not how the adults minister to students but how the *students* minister to one another.

Just as Jesus modeled peer ministry to His disciples, you are an ambassador of Christ equipping your students for peer ministry.

A man is never what he is in spite of his circumstances, but because of them.
OSWALD CHAMBERS

how to counsel a friend

starter

STORY PROBLEMS: Ask your group members to work with a few friends to list five steps a person might take to solve a problem. Briefly discuss the steps the group members brainstorm. While the answers will vary, the list should resemble something similar to the following:

1. Find the real problem
2. List ways to find a solution
3. Select a plan of action
4. Set up a way to be accountable for following your action plan
5. Determine a way to evaluate if your efforts are effective

Note: You can download this group study guide in 8½" x 11" format at **www.gospellight.com/uncommon/dealing_with_stress_and_crisis.zip.**

Now read the following story problem out loud or write it on a whiteboard:

You earn extra money mowing lawns. You mow 7 lawns in 2 hours, and you have 28 lawns to mow.

Ask the group members to apply their steps to solve this problem. (Note: If you find math intimidating, apply these principles to a specific task such as how to move a recliner or sofa from outside to inside—you might want to have props on hand to act out your solution.) Here is an example:

1. *Find the real problem.* The question you want to answer is how long it will take to mow 28 lawns.
2. *List ways to find a solution.* Here are some possibilities:

    (2 hours / 7 lawns) 28 lawns = solution

    28 lawns / (7 lawns / 2 hours) = solution

    $$\frac{2 \text{ hours}}{7 \text{ lawns}} \times 28 \text{ lawns} = x$$

3. *Select a plan of action.* Determine which equation to solve.
4. *Set up a way to be accountable for following your action plan.* One way to do this is set a time limit of 2 minutes to solve the problem.
5. *Determine a way to evaluate if your efforts are effective.* Solve and check your work. The answer for all equations is 8 hours.

Briefly discuss how having a plan for solving a problem promotes success or progress.

message

When faced with a crisis, most teens will turn to a friend for help. For this reason, being equipped to help your friends is vital, and it is essential to receive the guidance, wisdom and power of the Holy Spirit to help you. The following Scriptures and questions will help you develop a biblical perspective on peer ministry and counseling.

> *My command is this: Love each other as I have loved you. Greater love has no one than this, that he lay down his life for his friends. You are my friends if you do what I command. I no longer call you servants, because a servant does not know his master's business. Instead, I have called you friends, for everything that I learned from my Father I have made known to you. You did not choose me, but I chose you and appointed you to go and bear fruit-fruit that will last. Then the Father will give you whatever you ask in my name. This is my command: Love each other* (John 15:12-17).

1. What command does Jesus give to those who love Him?

2. How does Jesus say we are to obey this command?

3. What resources does Jesus give us to help us love each other?

4. According to these verses, how would Jesus describe the heart and character of someone who loves others? What is important to a follower of Christ?

But the wisdom that comes from heaven is first of all pure; then peace-loving, considerate, submissive, full of mercy and good fruit, impartial and sincere. Peacemakers who sow in peace raise a harvest of righteousness (James 3:17-18).

5. Godly wisdom can come directly from God as well as from a mature follower of Christ. What attitude does the person seeking godly wisdom have? What is the fruit of using godly wisdom in helping others?

And I will ask the Father, and he will give you another Counselor to be with you forever—the Spirit of truth. The world cannot accept him, because it neither sees him nor knows him. But you know him, for he lives with you and will be in you (John 14:16-17).

6. The guidance of the Holy Spirit, also called the Counselor and Spirit of truth, is available to all believers. When facing a crisis with a friend, how can the Holy Spirit help you?

All Scripture is God-breathed and is useful for teaching, rebuking, correcting and training in righteousness, so that the man of God may be thoroughly equipped for every good work (2 Timothy 3:16-17).

7. Scripture is another resource believers have to help a friend cope with a difficult situation. What does 2 Timothy 3:16-17 say are the benefits of knowing God's Word?

    _____

    _____

    _____

    _____

Therefore confess your sins to each other and pray for each other so that you may be healed. The prayer of a righteous man is powerful and effective (James 5:16).

8. Prayer is how you tap into God's power and keep yourself connected and "right" with God. How does James 5:16 say we can use prayer to help one another?

    _____

    _____

    _____

    _____

dig

Being an effective peer counselor means investing in your relationship with God through prayer, studying His Word, learning from mature believers and loving others. Consider how the following distinctions of effective peer counseling can equip you to effectively love others through a crisis and draw them closer to God.

1. Below is list of characteristics than effective peer counselors exhibit. Place an *X* in the box for the three or four distinctions you feel are the most essential.

   ☐ Depends on the Holy Spirit's power to counsel, comfort, guide and heal (see John 14:16-17).

   ☐ Uses the Bible wisely and appropriately as a guide to help people cope with their problems (see 2 Timothy 3:16-17).

   ☐ Connects with God regularly through prayer and is willing to pray for and with a person in need (see James 5:16).

   ☐ Desires to help others grow spiritually, know Jesus as Lord and Savior, and become more like Him (see Matthew 28:18-20; Romans 8:29).

   ☐ Seeks to become more Christlike, especially in developing goodness and love, knowledge of the Bible (see Romans 15:14), wisdom (see Colossians 3:16), maturity (see Galatians 6:12), and the spiritual gifts God has given him or her to help others (see Romans 12).

   ☐ Is sensitive to the counselee's attitude, motivations and desire for help.

   ☐ Works at building a genuine relationship with a person in crisis. Has good rapport and communication based on understanding, caring, being specific, being real, telling it like it is, and identifying what's really going on between the two of you. The Bible calls this "speaking the truth in love" (Ephesians 4:15).

   ☐ Is willing to use active listening and problem-solving skills to explore, understand and take action to help change problem thinking.

☐ Will approach a friend in crisis with flexibility, adjusting to the needs of the counselee and the problem (see 1 Thessalonians 5:14).

☐ Is teachable and willing to learn specific techniques or methods of counseling that are consistent with the Bible's teachings and values (see 1 Thessalonians 5:21).

☐ Develops cultural sensitivity and cross-cultural counseling.

☐ Builds skills in outreach and prevention. (For example, helping counselees connect with appropriate resources or community help and social support, including church and para-church groups.)

☐ Has an awareness of his or her own limitations and knows when and how to seek the help of others.[1]

2. Now list some ways a counselor can develop effectiveness in the areas you have checked. Compare notes with a friend.

3. Most peer counselors will have abilities in many of the areas listed, but few will have all of them. Why is this okay?

4. In 1 Corinthians 12:12-13,27, Paul says, "The body is a unit, though it is made up of many parts; and though all its parts are many, they form one body. So it is with Christ. For we were all baptized by one Spirit into one body. . . . Now you are the

body of Christ, and each one of you is a part of it." In what ways does the different gifts that Christians have enable them to effectively help those who are experiencing stress and crisis?

----

5. What are some resources in your area that you can take advantage of or refer a friend to for support in a crisis situation? How can you help a friend take advantage of these resources?

----

apply

We all have people in our lives that we influence. However, Christians have the opportunity to be an influence that draws people closer to Christ. No one else walks in our shoes or meets the people we you do in the circumstances they are experiencing at a certain moment in time. Every moment is a God-given opportunity that allows us to be a light for Christ in a particular circumstance.

what kind of personality do you have?

Every person is a unique instrument created by God. However, we tend to develop along the lines of similar personalities. For this reason, it's important to know your personality style in order to be a student leader and a peer counselor. The following survey will help you determine your personality style and also help you understand a bit about the personalities of others whom you may have the opportunity to help. Circle the letter that best represents your response for each statement.[2]

1. I like to . . .
   a. think fast and take charge of a situation
   b. think about complex things that most people haven't even considered
   c. listen to other people's problems and create a solution
   d. have other people need me

2. I like it when someone shows me he or she loves me by . . .
   a. surprising me with something
   b. letting me be myself
   c. hanging out with me, talking with me, or telling me how he or she feels
   d. doing things I've asked for

3. I like to give a friend . . .
   a. excitement and variety
   b. a chance to be independent
   c. love and compassion
   d. security

4. I like to . . .
   a. do things on the spur of the moment
   b. give people intelligent information
   c. keep everybody happy and make everybody feel included
   d. be someone others can depend on

5. You can count on me to . . .
   a. have "guts." I'm unafraid and strong
   b. be smart
   c. be understanding
   d. be responsible

6. I'm always looking for . . .
    a. excitement
    b. explanations
    c. peace
    d. order

7. The people who know me best would probably say I'm . . .
    a. competitive and ready to go for it
    b. quiet and organized
    c. emotional and sensitive to other people's feelings
    d. loyal—I follow the rules

8. I have a drive to be . . .
    a. free and allowed to do things spontaneously
    b. logical and on top of things
    c. accepted by other people
    d. in control of my little world

9. When I'm really down, I usually . . .
    a. lash out at people or act rude
    b. go off by myself or become really sarcastic
    c. cry or mope around
    d. feel sorry for myself

10. When I'm hanging out with friends, I usually . . .
    a. have a blast and enjoy myself
    b. mostly talk to one or two people
    c. make sure that everyone is having a good time and
        everyone feels included
    d. take charge when it's time to order the pizza or gather
        the funds for a movie

scoring

Add up all the As and write the total next to A below. Do the same for the Bs, Cs and Ds. The letter with the highest number of points best represents your personality style. Read the descriptions below to learn more about the personality God has given to you.

A: _____

B: _____

C: _____

D: _____

personality a

You love nothing more than simply having a good time! When it comes to trying something new, you possess energy you haven't even used yet—and that something "new" often involves performing in front of other people . . . or should we say showing off? (In a fun way, of course!)

Talent? You have a lot of it. You get bored fast, though, and you hate chores and school activities that involve a lot of drills and routines. You really like to do what you want and when you want, which makes it hard for you to follow rules and respect authority just because it's there. Your room at home and your locker at school probably won't win any prizes for neatness.

In the friendship category, you like people who are willing to try new things, and you have no problem taking the lead. You're a touchy-feely person, but you also like competition. Your friends can count on your off-the-wall surprises or your bizarre, spur-of-the-moment suggestions.

You learn best by experience, and you like to figure things out for yourself. In a nutshell? Life is a banquet, and you aren't going to go hungry!

personality b

You don't fit anyone's mold! You're always curious about how and why things work. You love the abstract, because you enjoy analyzing. When you're making a decision, it could take weeks! You're inventive, though, and if there's a new way to do something, you're the first one to try it . . . and then modify it.

You're very independent, and you don't show your emotions because you make decisions based on thoughts and facts, not feelings. You like having friends, and they know you love them, but you don't talk about it much. After all, they already know! You enjoy a challenge—especially in school—and you'll study for hours or weeks on a project as long as it's interesting to you. But drills and worksheets . . . forget it!

You don't automatically accept the rules; they have to make sense to you. Life is good because the possibilities are endless!

personality c

You love feelings! People often come to you with their problems because you love to talk about the way you feel and how they feel. You also have a great imagination! Because you hate conflict, you would rather have a root canal than confront somebody; but you love helping people get out of a bind and on the right track again.

You're definitely a romantic, so you tend to make decisions based on how you feel rather than on what you think. You're convinced that true love is out there and that it's possible to live happily ever after. People are your life, and the people in your life get flowers, poems, cards and notes from you. You absolutely *love* life and you're always looking for its real meaning.

You respond well to encouragement and approval, but you're not crazy about competition. You like things where everybody wins—there are no losers. You're deeply committed to your friends, your family and God. If there's someone most everybody loves, it's you!

personality d

If people want something done, they come to you because you're a rock. No matter how boring and detailed the schoolwork or job is, you stick to it until it's done. Even your P.E. locker is organized.

You respond to those in charge and have no problem following the rules. But you do have a problem when things get chaotic. You hate classes where the teacher has no control or parties where people go wild. You're a serious person. You show people you love them by doing things for them, like baking cookies for your boyfriend or doing the dishes for your mom when she's wiped out.

You know what's right and wrong and you live your life accordingly. Big changes make you nervous, and you feel guilty when you mess up (though that doesn't happen very often!). Though no one's perfect, you're pretty close.

analyzing the results

Remember, no single personality is better than another. God loves everyone He created. The important thing is for you to know and love who you are, because then you are able to strengthen your good points and work on your weak ones. This survey can also help you to understand what makes other people tick, which sure makes getting along a whole lot easier!

1. How close to your personality style did you feel the survey came?

    ----

2. Many people believe that teen-to-teen ministry is more effective than adult-to-teen ministry. Do you agree or disagree? Why?

    _____

    _____

    _____

    _____

3. Why is it sometimes difficult to counsel a friend effectively?

    _____

    _____

    _____

    _____

4. In 1 Thessalonians 2:8, Paul writes, "We loved you so much that we were delighted to share with you not only the gospel of God but our lives as well, because you had become so dear to us." How would you describe Paul's approach to ministering to others?

    _____

    _____

    _____

    _____

    _____

5. How could developing your skills as a peer counselor benefit you? What impact could it have on your relationships with your friends?

    _____

    _____

    _____

    _____

6. How could you minister to others more effectively?

reflect

1. Who are five people that you can name who have an influence in your life?

2. Who are your closest friends?

3. What is one situation in which a friend has looked to you for help in a time of crisis?

4. What skills were you able to use? What skills do you need to work on?

5. What can you do when you need help ministering to a friend in crisis?

    _____

    _____

    _____

6. Is there a peer who you look to for counsel? If so, who?

    _____

    _____

    _____

7. Who is an adult you can rely on for godly wisdom and advice when counseling a friend?

    _____

    _____

    _____

    _____

meditation

The way of a fool seems right to him, but a wise man listens to advice.
PROVERBS 12:15

Notes
1. Adapted from Joan Sturkie, *Peer Counseling in Youth Groups* (Grand Rapids, MI: Zondervan Publishing, 1992), p. 92. Used by permission.
2. Adapted from Nancy N. Rue, "What Kind of Personality Do You Have?" *Brio* 5, no. 10, October 1994, pp. 25-26. Used by permission.

how to listen
to a friend

I love the LORD, for he heard my voice; he heard my cry for mercy.
Because he turned his ear to me, I will call on him as long as I live.

PSALM 116:1-2

Tennessee. Arkansas. Oklahoma. Texas. New Mexico. Arizona. And finally California. After 2,900 miles, Mike and his friend finally crossed the border into California. Two and a half days of driving west—two and a half days of listening. What began as a series of phone calls from Mike in Tennessee eventually led his friend to catch a late-night redeye flight to Nashville.

A former student in a church high school and college ministry, Mike had joined the Army Reserves and moved to Nashville a year earlier. There he met a girl, and after only a couple of months of dating, they quickly got engaged. Two months later, the engagement was off and the relationship was over.

Mike was in trouble. Depressed. Possibly suicidal. He was drinking a lot and, worse, he was all alone. Alone with his thoughts. Alone with his pain.

When his friend arrived in Nashville, Mike wasn't proud of himself or his actions. He felt guilty for the serious mistakes he had made with his former fiancée. Never had he been so far from God or himself. Mike's life was a mess, and nobody knew that better than he did.

Mike didn't need a sermon, a few choice Scriptures or helpful advice from his friend. All he needed was for him to listen. So that's what he did. Two and a half days of driving and listening.

Whether you've been serving young people for years or this is your first week planning a youth Bible study, one of the most precious and valuable gifts you can give to your students is the gift of listening. Listening is the language of love, and when you listen to the thoughts, struggles and needs of teenagers, you are the ears of Christ to them.

Students won't be impressed by your biblical knowledge or life experiences if they don't sense you really care. Listening is a simple and specific way to show your love to them, and it is one of the most practical ways to demonstrate the love of God. Actively listening to students, whether they are in a serious crisis like Mike or just want a simple answer to a simple question, is an authentic demonstration of Jesus Christ. Young people will be more inclined to listen to God if you first listen to them.

No matter how good the communication, if no one listens all is lost.
The best communication forces you to listen.
MAX DEPREE

how to listen
to a friend

starter

COMMUNICATION BREAKDOWN: Play some loud music—two songs at the same time if possible—and have some snacks available as the group members arrive. As the music is playing, have a student volunteer read John 4:4-26 (without a microphone). Don't make any effort to get the other group members' attention. Then turn off the music and ask the students to share any details of the story your volunteer read. As needed, ask questions such as:

1. Who were the main characters?
2. What emotion was the person in the story feeling?
3. Did you sense any camouflaged feelings in the story?
4. How did you respond to what you heard?

After a few minutes, discuss the factors that made it difficult to understand what was happening in the story, such as it was difficult to hear, they didn't even notice the person was talking, or they were not interested in listening.

message

Good communication goes beyond hearing the words a person says or carefully choosing the words you speak. Communication means you effectively hear *and* respond to what someone else is sharing with you. Listening is key in communicating in a way that shows love, care and empathy—especially when someone is seeking help and comfort from you. Jesus gives us a great example of listening in John 4.

The Pharisees heard that Jesus was gaining and baptizing more disciples than John, although in fact it was not Jesus who baptized, but his disciples. When the Lord learned of this, he left Judea and went back once more to Galilee.

Now he had to go through Samaria. So he came to a town in Samaria called Sychar, near the plot of ground Jacob had given to his son Joseph. Jacob's well was there, and Jesus, tired as he was from the journey, sat down by the well. It was about the sixth hour.

When a Samaritan woman came to draw water, Jesus said to her, "Will you give me a drink?" (His disciples had gone into the town to buy food.)

The Samaritan woman said to him, "You are a Jew and I am a Samaritan woman. How can you ask me for a drink?" (For Jews do not associate with Samaritans) (verses 1-9).

1. What was the Samaritan woman trying to communicate to Je-
    sus through her words and actions?

    _____

    _____

    _____

> *Jesus answered her, "If you knew the gift of God and who it is
> that asks you for a drink, you would have asked him and he
> would have given you living water."*
>
> *"Sir," the woman said, "you have nothing to draw with and
> the well is deep. Where can you get this living water? Are you
> greater than our father Jacob, who gave us the well and drank
> from it himself, as did also his sons and his flocks and herds?"*
>
> *Jesus answered, "Everyone who drinks this water will be
> thirsty again, but whoever drinks the water I give him will never
> thirst. Indeed, the water I give him will become in him a spring
> of water welling up to eternal life."*
>
> *The woman said to him, "Sir, give me this water so that I
> won't get thirsty and have to keep coming here to draw water"*
> (verses 10-15).

2. How did Jesus respond to the woman to show He was listen-
    ing when she tried to tell Him that Jews do not associate with
    Samaritans? What did Jesus then say that grabbed her atten-
    tion and made her want to listen to Him?

    _____

    _____

    _____

> *He told her, "Go, call your husband and come back."*
> *"I have no husband," she replied.*

Jesus said to her, "You are right when you say you have no husband. The fact is, you have had five husbands, and the man you now have is not your husband. What you have just said is quite true."

"Sir," the woman said, "I can see that you are a prophet. Our fathers worshiped on this mountain, but you Jews claim that the place where we must worship is in Jerusalem" (verses 16-20).

3. How did Jesus show He was listening to the woman at this point? What did she say that indicates His words had an impression on her?

_____

_____

_____

Jesus declared, "Believe me, woman, a time is coming when you will worship the Father neither on this mountain nor in Jerusalem. You Samaritans worship what you do not know; we worship what we do know, for salvation is from the Jews. Yet a time is coming and has now come when the true worshipers will worship the Father in spirit and truth, for they are the kind of worshipers the Father seeks. God is spirit, and his worshipers must worship in spirit and in truth."

The woman said, "I know that Messiah" (called Christ) *"is coming. When he comes, he will explain everything to us."*

Then Jesus declared, "I who speak to you am he." . . .

Then, leaving her water jar, the woman went back to the town and said to the people, "Come, see a man who told me everything I ever did. Could this be the Christ?" They came out of the town and made their way toward him. . . .

Many of the Samaritans from that town believed in him because of the woman's testimony, "He told me everything I ever did." So when the Samaritans came to him, they urged him to stay with them, and he stayed two days. And because of his words many more became believers (verses 21-26,28-30,39-41)

4. What was the result of Jesus' conversation with the woman that simply began with, "Will you give me a drink?"

_____

_____

_____

5. How does this story demonstrate the importance of listening?

_____

_____

_____

_____

dig

Communicators often use a technique known as "echo" or "reflective listening" in which they restate the point they heard someone share with them to verify they truly understood what was said. Look at the story from John 4 again and evaluate Jesus' side of the conversation and how He used this technique.

1. How was listening an important part of Jesus' influence on the woman's life?

_____

_____

_____

2. In what ways did Jesus' responses show that He was listening
   to the woman and saw beyond her words?

   ----

3. How did this help Him guide the conversation and create the
   opportunity to address her need for eternal life?

   ----

4. How did the woman respond to Jesus' reflective listening
   technique and well-placed words? How did her response impact others?

   ----

5. Jesus' dialogue with the woman was a God-appointed opportunity. What does this say about the opportunities each of us
   have to point others to God and His gift of eternal life?

   ----

6. Jesus had God's insight when He counseled others. The Holy Spirit is available to each of us to help us see with God's eyes. How can prayer be part of preparing us to make the most of opportunities to listen to and help others in crisis?

_____

_____

_____

_____

apply

Reflective listening is a skill that you can practice and develop. It requires paying careful attention to a person's words and emotions, asking questions that guide you in understanding the context and meaning of what that person is saying, and an attitude of love and care that helps the person feel comfortable sharing his or her thoughts and feelings. Just as in Jesus' conversation with the Samaritan woman, a meaningful conversation often follows a progression from simple dialogue to addressing the heart of an issue. Here's an example of how a conversation between a peer counselor and a friend might begin:

Counselee: I hate math class, and my teacher is the worst.
Counselor: It sounds like you are really frustrated with your math teacher and the class.

1. What might the counselee say next?

_____

_____

_____

_____

2. How could the counselor then respond using reflection listening to move the conversation toward greater understanding and meet the needs of the counselee?

---

3. Practice the reflective listening technique with another person. Role-play the part of the counselee twice and role-play the counselor twice. What did you learn about listening to others?

---

4. What keeps most people from being good listeners?

---

5. Some people call listening "the language of love." Why do you think this is an appropriate description?

---

6. Who is someone you know who is an excellent listener? What does he or she do that makes you feel this way?

---

7. What are the results of this person's ability to listen?

_____

_____

_____

reflect

In Proverbs 18:13 we read, "He who answers before listening—that is his folly and his shame." Listening creates an environment of trust and opens opportunities to show love to another person.

1. Rewrite Proverbs 18:13 in your own words.

_____

_____

_____

2. Think of a time when you answered a person before really listening to him or her. How did your response affect the person sharing with you?

_____

_____

_____

3. What listening skills do you need to better develop? How could improving in these areas affect your relationships with friends and family?

_____

_____

_____

4. When is a time you need to have family or friends listen to you?

5. How does having someone listen to you make you feel about a difficult situation you might be facing?

6. Who do you know who might really need someone to listen to him or her? How can you start a conversation with that person?

Listening is as important a skill as giving good advice—and sometimes it is more important. So consider some ways you can actively listen to your friends and show them you love and care for them. Then prayerfully reach out and see where the conversation leads you.

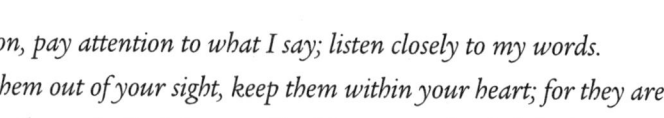

meditation

My son, pay attention to what I say; listen closely to my words.
Do not let them out of your sight, keep them within your heart; for they are
life to those who find them and health to a man's whole body.

PROVERBS 4:20-22

how to support a friend through loss

We were therefore buried with him through baptism into death in order that, just as Christ was raised from the dead through the glory of the Father, we too may live a new life. If we have been united with him like this in his death, we will certainly also be united with him in his resurrection.

ROMANS 6:4-5

"Some of you sitting in this room tonight will not live to see your twentieth birthday. Some of you will not graduate from college or ever get married. Look around the room. Some of your closest friends may not be alive a few years from now."

So went a youth pastor's challenge to a living room packed with high school students about choosing between life or death. The topic of death always seems to capture young people's attention. Although most people want to quietly ignore the idea of death, it seems to be a subject to which teenagers are surprisingly open. Students are willing to talk about death because it causes them to consider their decisions about life.

Your willingness to talk about the reality of death to students can be the bridge God uses to lead them to life in Jesus Christ. You can be God's instrument to help them understand what the Bible says about death, how to handle grief, what to say to dying relatives, and how to have hope in a world filled with death. You are in a unique position to challenge students to live life to the fullest.

Preparing this lesson on death and dying may prompt you to think about how death has affected you. Perhaps the simplest and most effective introduction to this sensitive subject is to share your personal experience of losing a loved one. Sharing how you dealt with feelings of grief, anger, sadness and loss can create a safe environment for students to share their feelings.

Allow this lesson to encourage and motivate you to rejoice in the life you have in Jesus Christ. Remember that Jesus has overcome death, sadness and dying. You can rejoice and be thankful that His life, death and resurrection were for your benefit.

No one ever told me that grief felt so like fear. I am not afraid,
but the sensation is like being afraid. The same fluttering in the stomach,
the same restlessness, the yawning. I keep on swallowing.

C. S. Lewis

how to support a friend through loss

starter

YOUR GRAVESTONE: The following may sound like a morbid activity, but it can actually be very meaningful. Ask your group members to think about what they would like to have printed on their gravestones. (The purpose for them in doing this that when people think about what they want their lives to represent when they die, it is easier for them to set priorities to accomplish their desired goals.) Here is an example of what they might want to put on their gravestone: "Here is a man who walked in integrity. He was deeply committed to his family and friends, and he was a positive influence for God's kingdom." Now have your group members try it.

Note: You can download this group study guide in 8^1/$_2$" x 11" format at **www.gospellight.com/uncommon/dealing_with_stress_and_crisis.zip.**

----

message

Our attitude toward death has a significant effect on our attitude toward life. Allowing our attitude to be inspired by God's truth will shape the choices and decisions we make now and for eternity. In this section, work with a friend or a group of three to four people to read what God's Word says about life, death and dying.

life is a gift

Our very breath and lives are gifts from God, so our attitudes should be that of thankfulness to God. Read the following verses and discuss how they relate to life being a gift to you from God:

> *This is the day the LORD has made; let us rejoice and be glad in it* (Psalm 118:24).

> *Praise him for his acts of power; praise him for his surpassing greatness . . . . Let everything that has breath praise the LORD* (Psalm 150:2,6).

> *But God demonstrates his own love for us in this: While we were still sinners, Christ died for us* (Romans 5:8).

What do these verses say about the attitude of the person who sees life from God's perspective?

----

life is eternal

Life on earth is but a snap of the fingers compared to eternity. Yet as we go about leading our lives, we often forget about the element of eternal life. Here is what the Bible has to say about eternal life:

> *For God so loved the world that he gave his one and only Son, that whoever believes in him shall not perish but have eternal life* (John 3:16).

> *I tell you the truth, whoever hears my word and believes him who sent me has eternal life and will not be condemned; he has crossed over from death to life* (John 5:24)

> *And this is what he promised us—even eternal life* (1 John 2:25).

> *God has given us eternal life, and this life is in his Son. He who has the Son has life; he who does not have the Son of God does not have life. I write these things to you who believe in the name of the Son of God so that you may know that you have eternal life* (1 John 5:11-13).

1. How has God made it possible for us to have eternal life?

    _____

    _____

    _____

2. How should the fact that life is eternal affect our hopes, dreams, fears, doubts and joys? Why is eternal life something to be desired?

    _____

    _____

    _____

there is hope

God brings hope to those who fear death. In John 14:1-3, Jesus says:

Do not let your hearts be troubled. Trust in God; trust also in me. In my Father's house are many rooms; if it were not so, I would have told you. I am going there to prepare a place for you. And if I go and prepare a place for you, I will come back and take you to be with me that you also may be where I am.

1. What words of reassurance does Jesus give His followers?

    ....

    ....

    ....

2. In 2 Timothy 1:10, Paul says, "The appearing of our Savior, Christ Jesus . . . has destroyed death and has brought life and immortality to light through the gospel." What does this verse say Jesus has done? Why is this good news?

    ....

    ....

    ....

3. Hope is the strongest weapon against the fear of death. In Titus 3:5-7, we read, "He saved us through the washing of rebirth and renewal by the Holy Spirit, whom he poured out on us generously through Jesus Christ our Savior, so that, having been justified by his grace, we might become heirs having the hope of eternal life." On what is hope of eternal life based?

    ....

    ....

    ....

God walks with us

It is important to remember that God walks with us through every situation we face in life, including its end. King David recognized this fact when he penned the words of Psalm 23:

> *The LORD is my shepherd, I shall not be in want. He makes me lie down in green pastures, he leads me beside quiet waters, he restores my soul. He guides me in paths of righteousness for his name's sake. Even though I walk through the valley of the shadow of death, I will fear no evil, for you are with me; your rod and your staff, they comfort me. You prepare a table before me in the presence of my enemies. You anoint my head with oil; my cup overflows. Surely goodness and love will follow me all the days of my life, and I will dwell in the house of the LORD forever.*

1. What does David say about walking "through the valley of the shadow of death"?

2. How does God walk alongside us when we are facing frightening situations?

3. How can you use this psalm to comfort those who fear death?

4. What are three phrases or ideas in this psalm that help remind you that God is with you? Write them in your own words.

_____

_____

_____

live life to the fullest

Realizing our time on this earth is limited should compel us to not waste it. So celebrate every heartbeat! In John 10:10, Jesus says, "The thief comes only to steal and kill and destroy; I have come that they may have life, and have it to the full." What do you think Jesus means when He say He wants us to have life "to the full"?

_____

_____

_____

dig

The Word of God can be a great comfort to those who belong to Christ, because it tells us that this life is not all there is—that there is a greater reward waiting for us at the end of our journey. Knowing God's Word and respecting it as eternal truth are key in experiencing comfort from it and in comforting others.

1. In your own words, what do the verses you have studied say about the reality of eternal life, the hope that Jesus offers, and how that hope impacts the life of a believer? (Try to limit your summary to five sentences or less.)

_____

_____

_____

2. How does a relationship with Jesus affect a person's perspective on death and dying (see 2 Timothy 1:10; Titus 3:5-7)?

_____

_____

_____

3. How does a biblical view of death affect a believer's attitude toward life and its challenges (see Psalm 23 and John 10:10)?

_____

_____

_____

Be joyful in hope, patient in affliction, faithful in prayer. Share with God's people who are in need. Practice hospitality. Bless those who persecute you; bless and do not curse. Rejoice with those who rejoice; mourn with those who mourn (Romans 12:12-14).

No one has ever seen God; but if we love one another, God lives in us and his love is made complete in us. We know that we live in him and he in us, because he has given us of his Spirit. And we have seen and testify that the Father has sent his Son to be the Savior of the world. If anyone acknowledges that Jesus is the Son of God, God lives in him and he in God. And so we know and rely on the love God has for us (1 John 4:12-16).

4. What insights can these verses provide to you when counseling a friend who is facing death in some way?

_____

_____

_____

5. In Hebrews 10:23-24, the author writes, "Let us hold unswerv-
    ingly to the hope we profess, for he who promised is faithful.
    And let us consider how we may spur one another on toward
    love and good deeds." How will confidence in the truth of
    God's Word equip us to help a friend experiencing grief?

---

apply

Undoubtedly, if you haven't done so already, you will one day experience the excruciating grief that comes when a loved one dies. The-
ologian Haddon Robinson described grief as "life-shaking sorrow
over loss . . . a dark, heavy thing, and hard to penetrate. The core of
the grief experience is anxiety."[1] In *A Grief Observed*, C. S. Lewis described the feeling of loss that accompanies grief in this way:

> In grief nothing "stays put." One keeps on emerging from
> a phase, but it always recurs. Round and round. Every-
> thing repeats. Am I going in circles, or dare I hope I am on
> a spiral? But if a spiral, am I going up or down it? How of-
> ten—will it be for always?—how often will the vast empti-
> ness astonish me like a complete novelty and make me say,
> "I never realized my loss till this moment"? The same leg
> is cut off time after time.[2]

understanding grief

As we help friends who are going through grief (or go through it
ourselves), we must remember the following important points:

- **Grief is normal.** We must grieve before we can go on with life. For this reason, we can't be afraid to cry or recognize our hurt. These feelings and emotions are normal.

- **Grief takes time.** We will not get over our pain instantly. The dull ache will be with us for a long time.

- **We need to talk about our hurt.** As we talk and share our sorrows, we will receive strength and mutual support.

- **There is comfort.** Reading verses in the Bible about peace, hope and victory over death can help.

Look up the following Scriptures. What comfort could they give to you or a friend during a time of grief?

Psalm 30:11-12

_____

_____

_____

_____

Psalm 46:1-3

_____

_____

_____

_____

Matthew 5:4

_____

_____

_____

_____

John 14:33

_____

_____

_____

1 Corinthians 15:51-57

_____

_____

_____

comforting others

In his book *The View for a Hearse,* Joseph Bayly describes the pain of loss he endured after one of his children died. He provides a beautiful illustration of how he received comfort from God during this dark time:

> I was sitting, torn by grief. Someone came and talked to me of God's dealing, of why it happened, of hope beyond the grave. He talked constantly, he said things I knew were true. I was unmoved, except to wish he'd go away. He finally did. Another came and sat beside me. He didn't talk. He didn't ask leading questions. He just sat beside me for an hour and more, listened when I said something, answered briefly, prayed simply, left. I was moved. I was comforted. I hated to see him go.[3]

1. The first person who spoke with Bayly said all kinds of positive things he knew "were true." So why did he wish the person would go away?

_____

_____

_____

2. Why did Bayly feel the second person was a better comfort to
    him in his grief?

    _____

    _____

    _____

    _____

    _____

3. Describe a time you have experienced grief or helped a grieving
    friend. What was comforting to that person? What wasn't?

    _____

    _____

    _____

    _____

    _____

4. Why do you think so many people have a hard time talking
    about death?

    _____

    _____

    _____

    _____

    _____

5. Why is expressing grief healthy? How can you help a friend
    do this?

    _____

    _____

    _____

    _____

6. How can your group encourage each other to be more honest with our feelings about death?

    ----

7. How can prayer be a key factor in effectively processing grief or helping a grieving friend?

    ----

reflect

1. In the space below, write a prayer to God telling Him your greatest fears about death and dying. You may want to write about your fear of your own death or the death of a loved one. Write about any doubts you have of eternal life or about your thankfulness for the assurance of your salvation.

    ----

2. Who would you turn to first for comfort when you are griev-
    ing? Why?

    _____

    _____

    _____

    _____

    _____

3. Why is it important to talk about your feelings concerning
    death?

    _____

    _____

    _____

    _____

    _____

4. What are some practical ways you could help when a special
    person in someone's life dies?

    _____

    _____

    _____

    _____

    _____

5. How can building a strong relationship with God help you ad-
    dress any doubts or questions you have about death and dying?

    _____

    _____

    _____

    _____

    _____

6. If you want to know more about starting or growing a relationship with God, who in your life can help you? (A Christian friend, a family member, a youth pastor?)

_____

_____

_____

_____

_____

meditation

I am the resurrection and the life. He who believes in me
will live, even though he dies; and whoever lives and believes in
me will never die. Do you believe this?

JOHN 11:25-26

Notes
1. Haddon W. Robinson, *Grief* (Grand Rapids: Christian Medical Society).
2. C. S. Lewis, *A Grief Observed* (San Francisco: HarperOne, 2001).
3. Joseph Bayly, *The View From a Hearse* (Colorado Springs, CO: David C. Cook, 1972).

HOME WORD

WHERE PARENTS GET REAL ANSWERS

Get Equipped with HomeWord...

LISTEN
HomeWord Radio

programs reach over 800 communities nationwide with *HomeWord with Jim Burns* – a daily ½ hour interview feature, *HomeWord Snapshots* – a daily 1 minute family drama, and *HomeWord this Week* – a ½ hour weekend edition of the daily program, and our one-hour program.

CLICK
HomeWord.com

provides advice and resources to millions of visitors each year. A truly interactive website, HomeWord.com provides access to parent newsletter, Q&As, online broadcasts, tip sheets, our online store and more.

READ
HomeWord Resources

parent newsletters, equip families and Churches worldwide with practical Q&As, online broadcasts, tip sheets, our online store and more. Many of these resources are also packaged digitally to meet the needs of today's busy parents.

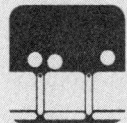

ATTEND
HomeWord Events

Understanding Your Teenager, Building Healthy Morals & Values, Generation 2 Generation and Refreshing Your Marriage are held in over 100 communities nationwide each year. HomeWord events educate and encourage parents while providing answers to life's most pressing parenting and family questions.

A Ministry with *Jim Burns*

In response to the overwhelming needs of parents and families, Jim Burns founded HomeWord in 1985. HomeWord, a Christian organization, equips and encourages parents, families, and churches worldwide.

Find Out More

Sign up for our FREE daily
e-devotional and parent e-newsletter
at HomeWord.com, or call 800.397.9725.

HomeWord.com

Small Group Curriculum Kits

Confident Parenting Kit

This is a must-have resource for today's family! Let Jim Burns help you to tackle overcrowded lives, negative family patterns, while creating a grace-filled home and raising kids who love God and themselves.

Kit contains:
- 6 sessions on DVD featuring Dr. Jim Burns
- CD with reproducible small group leader's guide and participant guides
- poster, bulletin insert, and more

Creating an Intimate Marriage Kit

Dr. Jim Burns wants every couple to experience a marriage filled with A.W.E.: affection, warmth, and encouragement. He shows husbands and wives how to make their marriage a priority as they discover ways to repair the past, communicate and resolve conflict, refresh their marriage spiritually, and more!

Kit contains:
- 6 sessions on DVD featuring Dr. Jim Burns
- CD with reproducible small group leader's guide and participant guides
- poster, bulletin insert, and more

Parenting Teenagers for Positive Results

This popular resource is designed for small groups and Sunday schools. The DVD features real family situations played out in humorous family vignettes followed by words of wisdom by youth and family expert, Jim Burns, Ph.D.

Kit contains:
- 6 sessions on DVD featuring Dr. Jim Burns
- CD with reproducible small group leader's guide and participant guides
- poster, bulletin insert, and more

Teaching Your Children Healthy Sexuality Kit

Trusted family authority Dr. Jim Burns outlines a simple and practical guide for parents on how to develop in their children a healthy perspective regarding their bodies and sexuality. Promotes godly values about sex and relationships.

Kit contains:
- 6 sessions on DVD featuring Dr. Jim Burns
- CD with reproducible small group leader's guide and participant guides
- poster, bulletin insert, and more

Tons of helpful resources for youth workers, parents and youth. Visit our online store at www.HomeWord.com or call us at 800-397-9725

HOME WORD
WHERE PARENTS GET REAL ANSWERS

Parent and Family Resources from HomeWord
for you and your kids...

One Life Kit

Your kids only have one life – help them discover the greatest adventure life has to offer! 50 fresh devotional readings that cover many of the major issues of life and faith your kids are wrestling with such as sex, family relationships, trusting God, worry, fatigue and daily surrender. And it's perfect for you and your kids to do together!

Addicted to God Kit

Is your kids' time absorbed by MySpace, text messaging and hanging out at the mall? This devotional will challenge them to adopt thankfulness, make the most of their days and never settle for mediocrity! Fifty days in the Scripture is bound to change your kids' lives forever.

Devotions on the Run Kit

These devotionals are short, simple, and spiritual. They will encourage you to take action in your walk with God. Each study stays in your heart throughout the day, providing direction and clarity when it is most needed.

90 Days Through the New Testament Kit

Downloadable devotional. Author Jim Burns put together a Bible study devotional program for himself to follow, one that would take him through the New Testament in three months. His simple plan was so powerful that he was called to share it with others. A top seller!

Small Group Curriculum Kits

Confirming Your Faith Kit

Rite-of-Passage curriculum empowers youth to make wise decisions...to choose Christ. Help them take ownership of their faith! Lead them to do this by experiencing a vital Christian lifestyle.

Kit contains:
- 13 engaging lessons
- Ideas for retreats and special Celebration
- Solid foundational Bible concepts
- 1 leaders guide and 6 student journals (booklets)

10 Building Blocks Kit

Learn to live, laugh, love, and play together as a family. When you learn the 10 essential principles for creating a happy, close-knit household, you'll discover a family that shines with love for God and one another! Use this curriculum to help equip families in your church.

Kit contains:
- 10 sessions on DVD featuring Dr. Jim Burns
- CD with reproducible small group leader's guide and participant guides
- poster and bulletin insert
- 10 Building Blocks book

How to Talk to Your Kids About Drugs Kit

Dr. Jim Burns speaks to parents about the important topic of talking to their kids about drugs. You'll find everything you need to help parents learn and implement a plan for drug-proofing their kids.

Kit contains:
- 2 session DVD featuring family expert Dr. Jim Burns
- CD with reproducible small group leader's guide and participant guides
- poster, bulletin insert, and more
- How to Talk to Your Kids About Drugs book

Tons of helpful resources for youth workers, parents and youth. Visit our online store at www.HomeWord.com or call us at 800-397-9725

HOME WORD
WHERE PARENTS GET REAL ANSWERS